William Edward Armytage Axon

Essays in Literature and Ethics

Edited With a Biographical Introd. by Wlliam E.A. Axon

William Edward Armytage Axon

Essays in Literature and Ethics
Edited With a Biographical Introd. by Wlliam E.A. Axon

ISBN/EAN: 9783337010461

Printed in Europe, USA, Canada, Australia, Japan

Cover: Foto ©Thomas Meinert / pixelio.de

More available books at **www.hansebooks.com**

ESSAYS

IN

LITERATURE AND ETHICS.

BY THE LATE REV.

WILLIAM ANDERSON O'CONOR, B.A.,

TRIN. COLL. DUBLIN,

Rector of SS. Simon and Jude, Manchester.

EDITED,

WITH A BIOGRAPHICAL INTRODUCTION,

BY

WILLIAM E. A. AXON.

MANCHESTER:

J. E. CORNISH,

16, ST. ANNE'S SQUARE, AND 33, PICCADILLY.

1889.

CONTENTS.

In Memoriam.

'Mid rough-hewn stones, a polished shaft he stood;
  His slender frame a cultured spirit shrined,
  Instinct with genius, vivid, thought-refined,
And consecrated to the highest good.
Rest in unrest he sought, found peace through strife;
  And all the wealth of his fine nature spent
  To serve his generation; well content
If he might help it to a nobler life!
We canonize Ambition; build to Fame
  Proud monuments that Time's attrition brave:
  What have we for the men whose life-works crave
An immortality of worth, not name;
No blot on their escutcheon? Pauper dole!
God sets them high upon his martyr-roll.

J. B. Greenwood.

INTRODUCTION.

THE following pages consist of selections from the literary remains of the late Rev. William Anderson O'Conor, and are fairly representative of his intellectual powers whilst not exhaustive of the material placed at the disposal of the editor. Should the present volume be received with favour, there are sufficient uncollected papers to form a second series. The volume owes its inception to the desire on the part of the members of the Manchester Literary Club and other admirers of Mr. O'Conor to have some permanent memorial of his powers as a critic. Most of the essays now republished were in the first instance read before the Club.

The editor's duties have been confined to the faithful reproduction of the text, and to the verifying, as far as possible, of the quotations. Some of the translations were, however, freshly executed by Mr. O'Conor for the essays in which they are found. It remains only to give some brief account of the remarkable man to whose memory this book is dedicated.

William Anderson O'Connor (for so his name was spelled originally) was a native of Cork, and was born there in 1820. His family came from the county of Roscommon, where they were important for generations. He was educated at Trinity College, Dublin, and took his B.A. degree in 1864. In a letter which appeared in the *Manchester Guardian* towards the close of 1885, Mr. O'Conor, in commenting upon Church matters, wrote :—

"When the clergy read of all the current taunts and insinuations about their 'pay,' I do not wonder that they turn away in silent and hopeless disgust from the whole subject. That disgust shall be overcome for once. Not one out of ten of us is 'paid' as the word is commonly understood. If we sought pay we should have gone to some other profession or business. All the early years of my life were given at a large pecuniary cost to the acquisition of knowledge assumed to be necessary for the discharge of a clergyman's office. I have never put the matter to myself as I now put it, but I now do ask, Can it be said that I have been paid for my work as a clergyman by having received £100 a year for the greater part of my clerical life? I remember well the countings of the cost with which I entered the Church. It was a giving up of the world, a surrender of its wealth and its prizes, and of the honours that might be won at the Bar or in the Army, with the sole understanding that I was to be freed from the anxieties of a secular calling, and maintained out of the Church's endowments, while I strove to do my Master's work. I speak of myself and allude to my motives simply because I am thus able to give a description that applies—I never uttered sincerer words than those I am now uttering—a hundred-fold more fitly to thousands and thousands of clergymen than it does to me. There are multitudes of clergymen to whom taking orders is equivalent to entering a monastery so far as seclusion from the sunny walks of life is concerned. No institution can be found that contains so many able and learned men, strong enough to move to the front rank in any worldly profession, and carry off the prizes, as may be found in the Church of England engaged in labours all their lives that might be called obscure and contemptible if they were not undergone in the service of One who washed His disciples' feet, and bade them to do to others what He had done to them. We are not paid or remunerated. We are merely supported out of endowments given to the Church for this very purpose by men who reflected that St. Paul worked with his own hands rather than be dependent on the offerings of those to whom he preached."

That this was emphatically true of Mr. O'Conor there can be no doubt.

His first appointment was that of lecturer on Latin at St. Aidan's College, Birkenhead; but in 1853 he was ordained by the Bishop of Chester, and became curate of St. Nicholas's Church, Liverpool, and afterwards of St. Thomas's, Liverpool. In 1855 he was appointed curate of the Church of St. Michael with St. Olave, Chester. He was in sole charge of this parish until 1858, when he became rector of St. Simon and St. Jude's, Granby Row, Manchester. This was his last preferment. On his settlement in Manchester, he soon became known as an eloquent preacher, and his reputation was further increased by the publication of a series of scholarly and earnest writings on theology. "Faith and Works" appeared in 1868, "The Truth and the Church" in 1869, "A Commentary on the Epistles to the Romans" in 1871, "The Epistle to the Hebrews" in 1872, "The Gospel of St. John newly Translated" in 1874, and "A Commentary on Galatians" in 1876. After completing his work on the "Fourth Gospel," Mr. O'Conor read Mr. Greg's "Creed of Christendom," and came to the conclusion that "many of the current objections to this Gospel stand in no relation whatever to its true meaning." In order that his readers might judge, he obtained permission to print Mr. Greg's vigorous attack as an appendix to his own work. The incident was creditable to both the scholars concerned. Another of these volumes is inscribed in these words: "To my tried and true wife, the companion and helper of my studies, for whose sake only has any thought of human praise ever mingled with my desire that 'the truth which makes free,' dear to her as to her husband, should prosper on the earth, this volume is dedicated."

Another department of literary activity now attracted Mr. O'Conor's attention. His "History of the Irish People" was evolved from a mere pamphlet, which appeared in 1876 and contained only Book I. For some time the project of its continuation remained in abeyance, but the increasing importance of the Irish Question in the minds of the British public led to the publication in 1882 of his "History of the Irish People" in two volumes, a work impressive not so much for wealth of erudition as for its beauty of style and its keen and searching ethical spirit. The book was dedicated to Professor F. W. Newman, with whom he was on terms of cordial friendship.

Mr. O'Conor was a man of marked individuality, and at times of morbid temperament. The voice of detraction was not silent, and the lack of deserved recognition undoubtedly injured a proud and sensitive spirit. But the best answer to any detractors on this account of one of the most lovable of men was furnished by his unceasing labour and wise counsel in many departments of public life. He was an active Guardian of the Poor for Chorlton. He was twice a candidate for the Manchester School Board—on one occasion suffering defeat, and on the other withdrawing in order to prevent a contest. As a condition of his withdrawal he claimed that an investigation should be made as to the propriety of the steps he had taken, with a view to the vindication of his character. The arbitrators then appointed justified his action.

He wrote but little in verse, but the quality of the following poem will justify the claim made for him of poetic instinct and expression; and it will also illustrate those points in his character and career to which allusion has been made.

CHILDE ROLAND LEAVING THE DARK TOWER.

You knew not your deity's needs,
Your gold-tinselled idol of clay,
If one truth-lover dared to disclaim:
False thoughts and false words and false deeds,
The plot and the fear and the shame,
Coward falsehood avoiding the day,
Whisp'ring slander, not daring to speak,
And all the mean shifts of the weak.

You knew not the signs of the times—
That the light can't be hid in the light—

That God's voice can outthunder man's crimes,
And a people's voice echo its might;
That a truth boldly spoken upfloats,
And flames like a beacon on high;
That a lie gasped by fifty hired throats
Is only a fifty-told lie.

You doomed me alive to the grave;
You buried me conscious and strong;
And you deemed that the sense of the wrong,
And the shouts of the prisoned who rave,
And the coffin-lid close o'er my head
Would make my free spirit your slave,
And rank me, the living, as dead.

But the heavens descending crushed in,
And earth rose to disburthen the sin,
And the grave burst asunder, and then
You, the keepers, became as dead men.

If the earth were an infinite cross,
And its socket the broad plain of hell;
And the fiends' multitudinous yell
Rose in triumph to blazon my loss,
And the universe reeled to the shocks
As you hammered my limbs to the rocks,
And the throb of o'ermastering pain
Rent each quivering sinew in twain—
No sense of dismay would intrude
On my soul's imperturbable mood.
I should smile on your night from my morn
With scoru—and scorn—and scorn.

Yes, I know I am God's lowest son—
The foolishest, feeblest, and worst;
But your malice has made me as first,

And your numbers have left me as one.
But I stand at the base of God's throne,
Disdaining concealment or guile,
Pursuing no end of my own,
Resigning my life to His smile ;
For He takes and He leaves for the Right :
And when others are armed for the fight
And the seeds which I ripen are sown,
If the earth needs my blood, so is best,
I will thankfully go to my rest.

He was equally popular as a speaker and as a preacher, and his racy wit, shrewd common-sense, lofty eloquence, and entirely original methods of thought made him a conspicuous and always welcome figure at many public gatherings. He was an active member of the Manchester Statistical Society, and contributed to its "Transactions." He became a member of the Manchester Literary Club in 1875, and at its social gatherings was seen at his best. He was tall and ascetic-looking, with a benevolent and intellectual aspect, and his wonderful flow of wit, humour, paradox, pathos, and high thinking made him a favourite with all. The cordial sympathy of his brother members not only consoled him, but the fellowship with other lovers of literature led him to deal with topics he might otherwise have passed by. His contributions to the "Papers" of the Club and to the *Manchester Quarterly* are marked not only by brilliance of style and paradoxical audacity, but by great critical insight, and by a really remarkable power of dealing with literature in its ethical aspects. In this spirit he touched upon such subjects as "From Lancashire to Land's End," "The Prometheus of Æschylus and Shelley," "The Relation of Religion to Literature," "The Prometheus Vinctus," "Wit and Humour," "The Book of Job," "Tennyson's 'Palace of Art,'" "Hamlet," "Browning's 'Childe Roland to the Dark Tower Came,'" "Reminiscences of Italy," etc. For several years he preached an annual sermon before the members of the Club assembled for the purpose at his church, St. Simon and St. Jude, Granby Row. One paper records his stay in Italy, where for a time he acted as chaplain to one of the Anglican churches in Rome. This change of scene would, it was hoped, have fully restored his strength, which had begun to fail, and on his return to Manchester he appeared to be in full physical and intellectual vigour. He was soon absorbed in work, preaching, lecturing, writing, and aiding every good cause that appealed to him for help. He determined to complete his "History of the Irish People." What had formed the two volumes of the original work was recast, and appeared as the first volume of a more popular issue. The second volume, bringing the history down to a recent date, was issued only a month before his death. When the MS. was ready for the printer a sudden illness compelled him to seek change at Torquay, and there he rapidly recovered. He came back to Manchester, and began to take up again the threads of his former busy, active life; but a recurrence of dangerous symptoms led to his return to Torquay, where he died on Tuesday night, March 22, 1887. The immediate cause of death was a second paralytic stroke. The following letter is from one who was with him to the end, and who had the best means of judging his character:—

"From the time of the last seizure I had very little hope. He never rallied after that, and the helplessness of his limbs and the loss of brain power steadily increased, till at last my prayer was that God would release him gently, and this was granted, for a more peaceful end could not have been—no struggle: we could scarcely say when he breathed his last. His gentle patience and his loving tender ways during that three months' quiet resting-time at Torquay were beautiful beyond expression. A purer spirit never entered into rest, I verily believe. Many will miss him. For myself, may God give me patience to wait till in His mercy I too may go home."

It is a just reproach to those in his district having influence and authority in the Church of England that they never officially recognised either the shining abilities or the high personal qualities of Mr. O'Conor, and that whilst men of inferior calibre, morally and mentally, had their due reward, no promotion was accorded to him, nor even such a position as would have enabled him to give his best to the cause of religion. No other communion having a man of his striking and peculiar genius would have been content to hide such a clear-burning and penetrating light under a bushel. It cannot be supposed that Mr. O'Conor himself was ignorant of this; doubtless he recognised it, although he did not resent it. The peculiarities of his temperament were such as would have disappeared with recognition and responsibility. He was a many-sided man, and in various sections of the busy community his loss will be deeply felt. It will be felt in the Church of which he was so distinguished an ornament, and wherever efforts are being made to promote the social good. He was, as I have said, one of the most conspicuous figures of the Manchester Literary Club, and whatever neglect—and there was neglect—there may have been in some quarters, there at least he had undivided admiration, and amidst the dark clouds that overhung some portions of his life, he derived consolation and inspiration from the sympathy that he could always count upon within the walls of the Club.

His was one of the old prophetic figures, and therefore perhaps somewhat strange and unaccustomed to our busy modern life. But the work he did and the counsel he gave was not less useful and not less needed than the words of those who in bygone ages were also voices crying in the wilderness. Very appropriate to his character and life are those lines in which an English poetess spoke of one of our English poets, who was also a prophet in his day:—

'Oh, men! this man in brotherhood your weary paths beguiling,
Groaned inly while he taught ye peace, and died while ye were smiling.'

There was in Mr. O'Conor that union of humour and deep melancholy that marked Cowper, as it has marked others of the prophetic race. It is this rare combination that gives them full sympathy with human joy and human suffering. Through much tribulation they attain to peace. So it was with him. He is now at peace—not in the green West, the land of his forefathers, nor in the dark and stormy North, where he had many sorrows and many consolations, but far away, stilled by the ceaseless music of the waves upon our Southern coast, beneath clear and lofty skies, and bathed by warm sunshine. Those skies are not clearer than was his intellect, nor loftier than his soul, and the sunshine is not warmer than was his loving heart.

ESSAYS IN LITERATURE AND ETHICS.

BROWNING'S "CHILDE ROLAND."

If on a first perusal of "Childe Roland" we are not induced, by a nameless fascination, to read it again, it is not likely, if we be led to do so by ordinary curiosity, that we shall find our perseverance rewarded by any fresh discovery. But if a startled and perplexed inner feeling recognises something old and familiar under its strange disguise—if a sympathy is awakened that takes the form of an almost personal recollection—a second and each repeated reading will give increased confirmation to that impression, until the belief is reached that there is here a true segment of the orbit of man's mysterious history, the key to romance, the comprehensive parable of all heroism, the poem of poetry itself. The problem or trial of life assumes the aspect in different poetic minds which constitutional taste or individual experience imparts to it. Tennyson—to whom disappointed affection stands as the representative sorrow—reproduces this idea in all his characteristic works. Finding in Shakspere a precious relic of old heart-religion kindred to his mood, he bowed himself in wrapt meditation before it, until there arose before his vision a vividly detailed picture of martyred love settling into the tranquil ecstasy of despair. The effort of a misanthropic ambition, struggling to conquer a world which it could neither join with in friendship nor part from in contempt, furnished Byron with the model according to which almost all his poems are constructed. It is the reality of an incessant strife and an ever-present failure in which we unconsciously participate that renders these fictitious sorrows so interesting to us. Here the explanation of modern poetry is to be sought. The poet is discovering his burthen and his mission. The baffled corsair and the unfortunate lover are types and adumbrations of a universal tragedy. But as the province of the poet becomes more clear his work seems to grow more obscure. The purely imaginative tale stood distinctly intelligible in its separate and independent perfectness. The typical narrative is made to lie so close to nature that it is encompassed in her mysterious shadow. Browning in "Childe Roland," also inspired by a single treasured note from the master of song, instead of suggesting the battle to which humanity is committed, by the fragmentary parallel of private sorrows, grasps the whole rounded scene at once, and describes it in circumstantial, if loosely-fitting, allegory. In "Paracelsus" he related a sad but not uncommon instance of imperfect aspiration and unsought attainment. The currents of imagination set moving during that composition, and the unused cosmic material that floated on them, seem to have given birth, by a purer because more intuitive poetic genesis, to the abstract ballad of Childe Roland.

There are some men—the most human because the most representative of that which distinguishes human nature—in whom the sense of what should be repels the contact of what is, and prevents it from impressing its maxims on the heart. The result is that they inevitably are in an attitude of inquiry and distrust towards all existing customs and beliefs. The race of man, whatever its origin may have been, always comprehended and has always been directed by the instinct of its final destiny. In working out this destiny it has many successive points of departure. Our kind is born anew whenever a soul of greater light is born. The being in whom moral perception first took shape was the pioneer of civilization and the archetypal knight-errant of romance. But he, in the primeval life of the cavern or forest, was not half so perplexing or disturbing a prodigy to the unregulated habits of his savage clan as the modern reformer, who would make the crooked straight and the rough ways smooth, appears to the fixed beliefs of his contemporaries.

Why is there so much suffering on earth? Is not the question answered by proposing another? Why is there so much settled formalized wrong-doing? It may be that the silencing explanation lies in some original taint of evil in our nature; but so long as there is in us enough of heaven to wonder at injustice and sorrow, and to yearn for sights of contentment and happiness, and so long as the creeds and laws of men are in agreement with the level doctrines of despair, and not with the holier insight, is it not open to us to think that most of the evils we witness are the result of man's lower nature usurping the government that belongs to the higher? Has not God given food for the body and dignity for the mind in sufficiency for all? and is it not law-established falsehood and vanity that are limited in supply?

It is likely, it seems to him who broods over these thoughts, that the remedy and the regimen are more in fault than the disease. Error canonized, legalized, deified, is the real source of the ills we suffer. How great and Godlike to drag forth the lurking Hydra, amidst the acclaim of a delivered universe, and exhibit him perishing under the arrows of Day! But there is no exulting hope no anticipated triumph, in the heart of him who, after long and wearying examination, is compelled to see that the Dark Tower, under whose shadow earth is ill at ease, is the boasted master-work of human wisdom, and that he who ventures to assail it must war against the convictions of his fellow-men. The nature of his study has been a solitary one. Unrelieved by personal joys, his spirit has been dwelling in the dark spots of history. In tracing the records of the past, and searching for the crowned lie that desolates life, he has grown bewildered and disheartened. A thousand doubts have arisen to darken his prospect. The aim of his youth remains, but it is dim and distant. The bright colours that lighted it have died out in the cold gray of the evening of life. The strong purpose still urges him forward, but the glow of early hope is dead, and its song is silenced for ever. The weary heart seeks rest even in failure, and reason cannot condemn the desire.

> I hardly tried now to rebuke the spring
> My heart made, finding failure in its scope.

His friends have been long censuring his infatuation and prophesying his ruin. They describe him as already lost. They speak of him and his search, in his presence, as if he were dead or absent, or so absolutely past reason and recovery that there is no longer any danger of wounding his sensibilities. The pursuit that is now his whole remaining life is to them a bitter jest. They associate him with all the fanatics who have attempted to make the world better than God meant it to be, instead of making the best of it for themselves. "He is one of the Band," they say; thus setting the matter beyond remonstrance, by placing him in a class that has ever been a byword of mockery with all men. He is so humbled in spirit that he is only aware of the affection that underlies their cruel taunts. He feels like a dying man whom his relations suppose to be already dead, and accordingly make their arrangements concerning his burial, in his hearing, in such a matter-of-fact way that the doubtful life remaining in him does not assert itself against their assured belief. So he resigns himself to his lot. All who entered on this enterprise have failed. That he sees. He is prepared to fail. But is he worthy? "All the doubt was now should I be fit?" When the youthful aspirant enters on the quest, there always mingles in his motives a disdain for those whom he condescends to serve. Paracelsus, in his early aspirations, expresses this stage of experience:

I seemed to long
At once to trample on, yet save mankind,
To make some unexampled sacrifice
In their behalf, to wring some wondrous good
From heaven or earth for them, to perish, winning
Eternal weal in the act: as who should dare
Pluck out the angry thunder from its cloud,
That, all its gathered flame discharged on him,
No storm might threaten summer's azure sleep:
Yet never to be mixed with men so much
As to have part even in my own work, share
In my own largess. Once the feat achieved,
I would withdraw from their officious praise,
Would gently put aside their profuse thanks.
Like some knight traversing a wilderness,
Who, on his way, may chance to free a tribe
Of desert-people from their dragon-foe;
When all the swarthy race press round to kiss
His feet, and choose him for their king, and yield
Their poor tents, pitched among the sand-hills, for
His realm: and he points, smiling, to his scarf
Heavy with riveled gold, his burgonet

Gay set with twinkling stones—and to the East,
Where these must be displayed!

Thus, in the intolerance of inexperienced ambition, the champion of virtue magnifies himself and the redress he means to achieve by vaunting the unworthiness of the recipients of his future bounty. It is a matter between him and mankind, and the worth of mankind must be consumed to feed the flame of his glory. The cause, the good work to be done, is merely the instrument that is to carve his greatness and his fame. It takes long years of protracted disappointment to teach him that the chief thing is the good of men, that men must always be viewed in the radiance of his hope, not fixed on himself, but making them seem deserving, that *he* is the instrument, and that the one deed required of him is the sacrifice of his glory as well as of himself. As this is the divinest act, the most unearthly dignity, it is only when it is revealed that the question of fitness arises. We never doubt our worthiness for vulgar rewards and prizes, because the motive is adequate to the end. It is the contrast between the selfish motive and the unselfish end that tears the veil from the past, and sends the questioner away to bury his dead, or to enter with greater light on a new career. Henceforth we have no fear for Childe Roland. His soul is wrought to the true heroic strain. It is not enthusiasm nor ambition that guides him, nor the impassioned rapture of the battle. It is that he has grown past the use of lesser things. Whether failure or success await him on earth, his triumph is secure. The end is gained. Truth has a true soldier.

His purpose fixed on, he turns from his friends to strangers for counsel and encouragement. "Cannot some redress be found, some deliverance wrought?" he asks one of that cynical tribe, the hangers-on of society, to whom the tragedy of life is laughter —one of those who cannot engage in the work of the world, but are willing to accept its alms, like beggars by the roadside, ready to shower hackneyed blessings on the robber's dole or the widow's mite, but full of hidden spite against the preachers of a manlier calling. "No redress?" is the tenor of his reply; "of course there is. The path to victory and fame lies before you. Blow your trumpet and the enchanted castle will fall. Go forward and conquer." The failure of the earnest is sweet to the place-hunter, who thrives on the vices of the community. Full of genuine envy of the pride and luxury of life—a portion of which is contemptuously dealt to him—he yet hates the champion of simple living and high thought. He would not save his patrons from destruction if he could, and yet he rejoices in the foreseen discomfiture of their assailant, because it is the sole justification of his own policy. Every noble effort that ends in disaster is a tribute to his wisdom. He cannot conceal his malignant joy at seeing another lover of men entering the toils, so he speeds him onward into the ominous tract of inquiry, where every step is perilous to the explorer. With a sinking heart the adventurer follows his instructions though aware of his treachery, and leaves the highway to traverse the region where common consent places the citadel of misrule. As he does so, the air around him seems to flush with a sudden recognition of his act.

> All the day
> Had been a dreary one at best, and dim
> Was settling to its close, yet shot one grim
> Red leer to see the plain catch its estray.

He is made to feel that he has committed himself by seeing that the indifference of men is changed for a moment into scornful attention. That attention is deliberate desertion, at the very moment when he most stands in need of countenance and help.

For mark! no sooner was I fairly found
  Pledged to the plain, after a pace or two,
  Than, pausing to throw backward a last view
O'er the safe road, 'twas gone; grey plain all round:
Nothing but plain to the horizon's bound.
  I might go on: nought else remained to do.

He is abandoned by men and the institutions of men. The safe road is the way of the crowd, the path of conventionality. You may outrage every principle of honour and equity without losing the world's friendship. You may violate in spirit or by open transgression any particular law, and, provided you win by so doing whatever the world prizes, you are secure in the world's applause. But undervalue the ends towards which law is directed—revolt against the prevalent fashion—assail the world's respectability—neglect its standards—or speak ill of its gods—and you are lost. You have missed your way past recovery.

Better to err amid the throng
Than boldly speak ten thousand wrong.

The "hateful cripple" is safe by the highway but Childe Roland has no path to follow. He held law to be unjust, or religion to be corrupted, or the general aim of society to be somehow mistaken. This is leaving the highway, and simply doing this, he is abandoned to an unbounded trackless plain. When he quitted the road it ceased to exist for him. His departing from it means that his respect and value for it ceased. The change was inward in his feelings as well as outward in the conduct of men towards him. The man who walks by abstract right walks in a solitude. Right, apart from custom, has beaten no visible path. So when a man wishes to walk higher than others who walk in the safe road he must go alone. Take down the conventional signposts of church or party and you create a wilderness, until you obtain followers enough to make a road. And, moreover, in a society whose wealth is balanced by poverty, the moment you ignore the artificial greatness and excellency, the moment you take away or cease to regard the gilding that pleases the eye, the whole dignity and worth of the social fabric vanishes. Take away, or cease to value, the imponderable refinement, the shifting hue of fashion, the pride that apes worth, and the remainder seems an untold grossness. Remove out of the account the blossom or the fruit that gathers all the sun's splendour to itself, and you have the heavy crawling stem, the gnarled, ungraceful joints, and the roots that toil in everlasting darkness. Look at the palace and the hovel together, and your eye and thought may find partial relief. There is a balance of some sort, a counterpoise, a deliverance answering to a sacrifice. But lose sight of the palace, which, if you are thinking how to assuage the miseries of the hovel, you cannot help doing, and what is left!

I think I never saw
Such starved ignoble nature; nothing throve:
For flowers—as well expect a cedar grove!

. . . .

No! penury, inertness, and grimace,
In some strange sort, were the land's portion. "See,
Or shut your eyes," said Nature peevishly,
"It nothing skills: I cannot help my case:
'Tis the Last Judgment's fire must cure this place,
Calcine its clods, and set my prisoners free."

If there pushed any ragged thistle-stalk
Above its mates, the head was chopped; the bents
Were jealous else. What made those holes and rents
In the dock's harsh swarth leaves, bruised as to baulk
All hope of greenness? 'tis a brute must walk
Pashing their life out, with a brute's intents.

As for the grass, it grew as scant as hair
In leprosy; thin dry blades pricked the mud,
Which underneath looked kneaded up with blood.
One stiff blind horse, his every bone a-stare,
Stood stupefied, however he came there;
Thrust out past service from the devil's stud!

Alive? he might be dead for aught I know,
With that red, gaunt, and colloped neck a-strain,

And shut eyes underneath the rusty mane;
Seldom went such grotesqueness with such woe;
I never saw a brute I hated so;
He must be wicked to deserve such pain.

This description answers to almost any piece of ground in the suburbs of a large town, where nature has been invaded and art has not yet made progress in her substitutions. The despoiled surface, the enforced barrenness, the bruised weeds, and the lean and starved horse, are familiar objects in such a locality, and are all full of startling symbolism to a temper that desponds over human prospects. There is a stage of transition in the advance of society that resembles this incomplete victory over the region of spontaneous growth. As the poisoned breath of the city kills the surrounding herbage, so does the first contact of civilization distort the rectitude of nature. When culture begins to move the soil, weeds spring up, or what once seemed flowers now seem to be weeds. The virtues of primitive life and of civilization appear in an unsightly form in the middle state, when removed from their native setting, and not yet enlarged to heroic proportions. The village Hampden has his proper dignity when withstanding the little tyrant of his fields, as the historic Hampden has when resisting the usurper of his country's rights. So with the "mute, inglorious Milton" and the "guiltless Cromwell." But there is a tract of progress where only the meanness of these characteristic qualities is visible. This is the sphere where the knight of modern romance labours. We have to remember that our passions seem ignoble only when engaged on ignoble things, and that they are inevitably so engaged with the mass of men. The jealousy that ennobles when it inflames a national contest, or watches the encroachments of a foreign tyrant, is pitiful when it embitters the humble aspirant for fame or fortune, or tempts one son of misery to look askance on some slight accession to the joys of his struggling neighbour. The stately pleasures of the great also take away, in some unintentional manner, from the grace and beauty of the toiling man's happiness. "Seemeth it a small thing unto you to have eaten up the good pasture, but ye must tread down with your feet the residue of your pastures? and to have drunk of the deep waters, but ye must foul the residue with your feet? And as for my flock, they eat that which ye have trodden with your feet; and they drink that which ye have fouled with your feet" (Ezekiel xxxiv. 18, 19). But however we may philosophize on the subject, it is one that fills the heart of him who is absorbed in its details with kindred desolation. Agonized nature seems to him to yearn for a fresh creation, and he is ever confronted with that crowning wrong that makes the sufferer appear to be worthy only of suffering.

I shut my eyes and turned them on my heart.
As a man calls for wine before he fights,
I asked one draught of earlier, happier sights,
Ere fitly I could hope to play my part.
Think first, fight afterwards—the soldier's art;
One taste of the old time sets all to rights!

Not it! I fancied Cuthbert's reddening face
Beneath its garniture of curly gold,
Dear fellow, till I almost felt him fold
An arm in mine to fix me to the place,
That way he used. Alas! one night's disgrace!
Out went my heart's new fire and left it cold.

Giles, then, the soul of honour—there he stands
Frank as ten years ago when knighted first.
What honest man should dare (he said) he durst.
Good—but the scene shifts—faugh! what hangman hands
Pin to his breast a parchment? his own bands
Read it. Poor traitor, spit upon and curst!

The hero of conventional romance closes his eyes or stops his ears to shut out the sights and sounds of threatening or seduction that attend him as he goes to assail the enchanted castle that holds some captive princess. Childe Roland has no such relief or immediate prospect to inspirit him. The future veils itself from his hopes in impenetrable gloom. Launched on his career in the light and warmth of early enthusiasm, when Fancy strewed the path of duty with roses and filled the air with the voices of acclaiming crowds, he is now compelled to proceed in darkness, silence and solitude; urged forward only by the impetus and following the direction of that happier day. Why can he not take refuge from the depressing effects of his present experience in recollections of the past? Why can he not surround himself with the associates of his youthful aspirations? The attempt is vain. His heart has lost the vision of brightness. The firmament of his memory is without sun or star. He first recalls the image of the most genial and affectionate of his comrades till he almost pauses, as of old, at the clasp of his detaining arm. But the blackness rises between them as he remembers the sudden disgrace that blighted his friend's career before his fame was made. He then thinks of another, sanguine and daring, and pledged to the path of honour. Oh, but the end of it! That friend died the death of a traitor, and his very followers could not wholly protest against his doom.

> Better this present than a past like that;
> Back therefore to my darkening path again!

The Present requires all his energies. The objects that come under his view are of more moment than bygone dreams. It is part of his quest to note the things he sees.

> A sudden little river crossed my path
> As unexpected as a serpent comes.
> No sluggish tide congenial to the glooms;
> This, as it frothed by, might have been a bath
> For the fiend's glowing hoof—

This stream, "so petty yet so spiteful," the Lethe of the level wretchedness of life, the Nile of the Egypt of the hopeless, nourishes whatever vegetation is possible in such a wilderness.

> Low scrubby alders kneeled down over it;
> Drenched willows flung them headlong in a fit
> Of mute despair, a suicidal throng:
> The river which had done them all the wrong,
> Whate'er that was, rolled by, deterred no whit.

While fording it he fears to "set his foot on a dead man's cheek," and as he fathoms it with his spear a cry, like the shriek of an infant, issues forth. When he gains the other bank, he comes on a spot where some wild inhuman contest had been waged. It was no orderly anticipated battle of trained soldiers. The place must have created the combatants. The exhalations of the river must have inspired their frenzy. No such creatures as writhed and struggled here ever came from any other domain of nature.

> No foot-print leading to that horrid mews,
> None out of it. Mad brewage set to work
> Their brains, no doubt. .

A little farther he finds an engine which his boding imagination transforms into an instrument of torture. The twin expedients of hell for the prevention of the growth of man's moral consciousness have been the oblivion of the poisoned brain and the terrors of law—drunkenness and the gallows—the bath for the "fiend's glowing hoof" and "Tophet's tool."

> Then came a bit of stubbed ground, once a wood,
> Next a marsh, it would seem, and now mere earth
> Desperate and done with.

There is no room for further effort, no possibility of success. Every attempt has been made, every variety of expedient has been tried, and all has been done to prove this result. In this the prospects of humanity culminate. The world is only "mere earth, desperate, and done with."

And just as far as ever from the end!
 Nought in the distance but the evening, nought
 To point my footstep further!

Suddenly, aroused by no audible challenge, but somehow recalled to himself by a sound, a tremor, a shadow, a thing of darkness and the air, an impalpable shape that floats like a bird of evil omen, spontaneous, effortless, through the deepening twilight, he becomes aware that he is no longer in an open plain, free to continue his journey or to retire. He had seen no mountains as he advanced, yet now they surround him. The level must have lifted itself in an angry convulsion on all sides of him. The horizon is hemmed in by frowning heights, which a moment before were invisible. The community, the whole mass of men and laws and beliefs, which he had been surveying, criticising, condemning, seem, like billows of an angry sea, to overwhelm him. He had been seeking amidst the ruins of human happiness for the stronghold of the destroyer, and now, unexpectedly, he is encompassed by its walls. An instant's reflection, and the truth flashes on him. He is captured by the enemy whom he has been all his life seeking to discover and attack. He who assails or even suspects the integrity of the social arrangement, and searches through it for the influence that wields the power of harm, never makes the discovery till he is entangled in its strongest meshes. That influence is ever cautiously watching him. It sees his mistrust while it is forming in his conscience. It gathers his secret purposes from the glance of his eye and the measure of his step before his lips have spoken. It rises to meet him. The eminences and elevations which he had ignored appear behind and before, threatening him, so that he is put upon a hopeless defence instead of being able to assail. "Where are the falsehoods and tyrannies that mar the hopes of men?" he had said. Instead of replying, they silently and darkly crush their enemy. He finds the Hydra only when its folds are tightening round his every limb, and its poison is mingling with his breath.

Looking up, aware I somehow grew,
  'Spite of the dusk, the plain had given place
  All round to mountains.

. . . .

Yet half I seemed to recognise some trick
  Of mischief happened to me, God knows when—
  In a bad dream perhaps. Here ended, then,
Progress this way. When, in the very nick
Of giving up, one time more, came a click
  As when a trap shuts—you're inside the den!

Burningly it came on me all at once,
This was the place!

. . . .

What in the midst lay but the Tower itself?
The round squat turret, blind as the fool's heart,
Built of brown stone, without a counterpart
In the whole world. The tempest's mocking elf
Points to the shipman thus the unseen shelf
He strikes on, only when the timbers start.

All his hopes are frustrated, all his calculations put out. His long self-discipline has been in vain. His long preparations are useless against an unforeseen danger. He had not thought about himself, but it is against him that every weapon is now directed. The meanness and dull shallowness of the attack take him unawares. He had thought of a brave and honourable opposition; he finds only spite and vindictive malice. He supposed he was fighting against the greatness of institutions; he finds the smallness of men. The greater the end a man has in view, the lower and more degrading is the conflict in which he must engage. A soldier in arms meets a soldier in arms. A soldier of truth meets a hireling of falsehood. This is the nature of the case. The Satan of Milton has misled us. In whatever pomp and pride evil may array itself, resistance brings out its ignoble nature. This is the justification and should be the encouragement of the contest. The greatness of heaven battles against the littleness of earth, because it is littleness. Childe Roland, when he knew that his own life must be the forfeit, thought at least of falling in equal fight in the open day, with some ray of glory radiating from his knightly armour. But he had made no provision, taken no forethought, against "the round squat turret, blind as the fool's heart." He sees, in his newly-awakened perception, his foes rousing themselves indolently to feast their eyes on his torture. At the instant when all the vigour of his soul is required, he is paralyzed by the crowding memories of the failures of all who came there before him. None of them ever escaped. He is caught in the machinery of a merciless fate. What are strength or fortitude or good fortune against the iron blow that crushes the limbs of the wretch extended on this wheel of destiny? All his predecessors have fallen. Their shadows haunt the place.

There they stood, ranged along the hill-sides, met
  To view the last of me, a living frame
  For one more picture! in a sheet of flame
I saw them and I knew them all.

He must become as one of them. It is all that remains for him. No, something more remains!

He is not without his victory and his note of triumph. He has discovered the Dark Tower, and, so far as his breath can avail, the world shall know of his discovery. He will let his challenge of defiance to his enemy, of alarm to the slumbering world, ring through the muffled stillness, and fall only after the due forms of honourable combat.

> And yet
> Dauntless the slug-horn to my lips I set
> And blew "*Childe Roland to the Dark Tower came.*"

Nothing succeeds like success, men say. Yea, rather, nothing succeeds like failure. Success succeeds in personal gain for a few. Failure succeeds in the eternal triumph of right for all!

TENNYSON'S "PALACE OF ART."

It is commonly said that there is no waste in creation, and that the displacement of an atom would unsettle the balance of the universe. This is true only in a metaphysical relation. In the external world, so far as our power of observation can reach, waste is the rule, use the exception. Our earth during unnumbered ages was a wilderness. Even now its inhabited and cultivated portions are only islands and oases. The interplanetary spaces teem with fragments of worlds which are apparently as useless as the dust of our globe would be if it were blown about for ever by the winds. Every life of plant and animal is rescued from the midst of countless failures. Every creature that moves in densest shoal or flock is also the centre of a ruined region of unreached existence. All organization is only a germ in a gigantic involution of unproductive expenditure, a minute kernel in a colossal integument of sterility.

Is this apparent waste real? Does this superfluity exist in vain? Nature is what it is—in its immensity, its variety, its redundancy—for the sake of man. The soul of man is the reflection of the outside world; and that it may be multifarious, vast, infinite in inexhaustible resources, affluent in unconceived possibilities, nature is so. God does His work with boundless margin, that man's soul may expand and soar as in unlimited space. There is no waste in the lavish prodigality of matter, time, and space, because it only provides a field wide enough for the imagination to traverse. Man does not live on bread alone. The desert places are more fertile than the blossoming garden or the yellow field of corn. That which is limited and practical in man is the shadow of earth's symmetry and organization; all that is sublime in him is the gloom of her barrenness and deformity. If the elements put forth just so much force and material as was needed for the designed effect, if there was an accurate proportion always between the effort and the product, every exertion of the human will would be narrowed to a calculation in arithmetic. Man would repress his power to visible and definite ends, and nothing would be left for aspiration. Exact law is ever lost in some undefined principle whose orbit is beyond our vision, and even our measured actions have a meaning whose echoes are heard in the pathways of the stars.

The indefiniteness of the universe is reproduced in us. Our thoughts swell beyond the compass of possible achievement. Our desires outstrip our knowledge. Our distinct conceptions are fertile spots amid wildernesses of vagueness and obscurity. The waste of light in morning dawn and evening sunset, the waste of genial warmth as summer is slowly killed by cruel winter, the waste of consciousness as we pass dimly into the darkness of sleep, all leave their impress upon us. Wonder, awe, mystery are the perfumes of the flowers that never bloom, the echoes of the voices that never become articulate, the impalpable sway of the uncreated creation. Our faculties melt into the immeasurable. Language imitates the extravagance of nature, and spreads into hyperbole and rhetoric. Belief is surrounded by an infinitude of mental space, which we call doubt; but which, in truth, is the field of progress and of action, the atmosphere of light and life, the breathing-place of mental health. God risks our loyalty to Him to make us ceaseless in our pursuit of truth. Indetermination of aim answering to Nature's vastness, her eternity, her infinity, her stores of wealth too great for any known end, gives birth to poetry. We can see the spendthrift outlay of creation bearing fruit in local and national life. The industry of a district is arrested to save a fellow-being from death. The nation puts forth thirty million hands to rescue one or two captives from a savage. Such is the connection between man's soul and the outer world. Art in its æsthetic sense undertakes to embody, to arrange into rule, and to mirror back on the soul, its own grandeur, its own ever-widening universality, imprinted upon it by the universality of external nature. The first duty, therefore, of art is to be true to Nature's ends, and not to detain man's soul in a reverie of idle delight, but to speed it onward to the one far-off divine event to which the whole creation moves. The surface of the soil may be divided into personal possessions; men or nations may call the lands after their own names; the mountain, the ocean, the cloud, the desert isle, the very planet, may have some imaginary shackle of ownership flung upon it: with these appropriations and limitations art has nothing to do. It must deal with nature in those influences which are the inalienable heritage of mankind. Earth in her wholeness, the heavens in their unfathomable depth, and the sublimities of genius were made common property for all. When God formed man in His image He committed the development of the likeness to impressions daily growing from the divine frame of the universe. He placed him amidst scenes of bold and historic magnificence that he might imbibe their colours and magnitude. The end of art is to help nature in imprinting the likeness of God on the soul of man.

In the "Palace of Art" we see a being who has trained himself to catch all that is beautiful or touching in nature and history, and employ it for his own solitary gratification. He has sifted the bow from the shower, the grateful terror from the danger and the pain, the kindling emotion from the agony and despair, the sublime from its toil, the heroic from its sacrifice. The cries of earth are mellowed to music before they reach his ears, and the writhings and contortions of its combats are idealized into attitudes of grace. Nature's convulsed career amuses him with a phantasmagoric show, while he dwells beyond the reach of her attractions.

> I built my soul a lordly dwelling-house
>   Wherein at ease for aye to dwell.
> I said, "O soul, make merry and carouse,
>   Dear soul, for all is well."

. . . .

And "while the world runs round and round," I said,
"Reign thou apart, a quiet king,
Still as, while Saturn whirls, his steadfast shade
Sleeps on his luminous ring."

The design of the architect of this psychic palace was to enlarge his capacity of enjoyment, to garner for himself the whole harvest of beauty, and to eat, drink, and be merry on goods laid up for many years. It is not the account of an artist whose personal life is untouched by his art. There have been painters and poets who worked with sunbeams while their lives were of the darkness. There have been philosophers and logicians who constructed deathless systems while their steps trod ceaselessly in the labyrinth of error. There have been orators who transmitted truth to posterity in sentences of flame, but on whose pledged promises their contemporaries could place no reliance. There have been moralists whose maxims were like glittering insects engendered in impurity. There have been preachers whose accurate balancing of dogma protected the perfection of their worldliness, whose spiritual unction could only supply fuel for a fiercer fire of remorse than natural depravity can kindle. But all these did a finished work, and left contributions to a future which they neither foresaw nor desired.

The case here presented is different. It is that of a favoured and richly-endowed being, calm, self-possessed, refined, who, with discernment to choose and power to execute, out of nature's strength gathered sweetness for himself, and luxuriously fed his soul on the visions which dying men saw through their tears. It is as if the vapours, rejoicing in their elevation, should never descend to fertilize the plain out of whose arteries they had arisen; as if Liberty, the child of agonies wide as the world, deep as the heart, should gain her apotheosis to shine like a star in settled splendour over a despot's throne; as if Truth, transformed from her ancient servitude and bursting from mediæval disfiguration, should soar to the higher regions of heaven to company with angels, and never bless with her loveliness the race from whose travails she had sprung.

> A huge crag-platform, smooth as burnished brass,
>   I chose. The ranged ramparts bright
> From level meadow-bases of deep grass
>   Suddenly scaled the light.
>
> Thereon I built it firm. Of ledge or shelf
>   The rock rose clear, or winding stair.
> My soul would live alone unto herself
>   In her high palace there.
>
> Four courts I made, East, West and South and North.

Let us contrast for a moment with this unscaleable, impregnable, entranceless fortress of unsocial refinement and uncommunicated joy, the divine idea that warmed the hearts of men of a former time, whose inspired labours have all but shared the fate of ordinary struggles for the good of mankind, and been diverted from ministering to the elevation of the multitude to giving a zest to the pleasures of the chosen few. "And I saw a new heaven and a new earth . . . and I saw the holy city coming down from God out of heaven. And I heard a great voice out of heaven saying, Behold the tabernacle of God is with men . . . and God shall wipe away all tears from their eyes . . . And there came unto me one of the seven angels . . . and he carried me away in the spirit to a great and high mountain, and showed me that great city descending out of heaven from God . . . and it had a wall great and high and had twelve gates . . . on the east three gates; on the north three gates; on the south three gates; and on the west three gates . . . and the gates of it shall not be shut at all by day: for there shall be no night there."

The internal construction of the palace—which throughout the Poem is now the symbol, now the actual creation of a frame of mind, a material erection and a mental disposition acting and reacting on each other—reproduces in an artificial form the grand features of natural scenery. Four floods of fountain foam pour from the golden gorge of dragons. Cloisters, branched like lofty woods, echo to the waterfalls. A gilded gallery shows the distant ocean. The ancients, who believed that superhuman beings dwelt in the fountain and the tree, held in their own way the certain truth that the Godhead speaks to man's soul from the augustness and the tenderness of nature. In the artistic rendering and the æsthetic perception, the beautiful imagination of indwelling deity is imperilled. The God of heaven will not deign to dwell in temples made with hands, nor will the God of nature unconditionally suffer His glories to be enclosed within human adaptations.

> Quanto præstantius esset
> Numen aquæ, viridi si margine clauderet undas
> Herba, nec ingenuum violarunt marmora tophum.
>
> *Juv. Sat.* iii. 18.

But it is not in the temple or the palace of material architecture that God refuses to make His abode, but in the soul of the worshipper that is walled in by symbols, that loads itself with God's gifts, clothes itself in His beauty, arms itself with His power, and sullenly refuses to be governed by His all-embracing love.

The latent and unloving spirit of exclusiveness reveals its tendency as we proceed to the exterior aspect of the building. The four currents mingle in one stream, and as they rush over the mountain's side form a rainbow. And on each pinnacle of the palace, instead of chimneys, statues standing on tiptoe tossed up clouds of incense from golden cups.

> So that she thought, "And who shall gaze upon
> My palace with unblinded eyes,
> While this great bow shall waver in the sun,
> And that sweet incense rise?"

The delicate disguises and graceful dissemblances of art, if confined to a class, engender a fictitious sense of superiority. Every device that distinguishes the common wants of men, their common dependence on the bounty of nature, raises barriers more insuperable than any legal privilege could create. The very fabric of the mind becomes imbued with a different colour. In concealing the homeliness of our wants, we dissever our brotherhood. Because we drape our daily needs in elegance, we suppose that they are not the same as the urgent necessities of the uncultured man. A coronet and ermine cannot, we imagine, be intended to shelter their wearer from the cold in which ordinary humanity shivers. The dainty appetite that fares sumptuously off golden dishes cannot be of the same quality as the hunger which is solaced by a crust eaten from the hand. The disease that is mysteriously withheld from the vulgar ear and announced in formal bulletins cannot be that which brings trembling into the toiler's home.. The demise that ceremoniously visits the palace, and with respectful pomp conducts its charge to a palatial mausoleum, cannot be the same death that invades the cottage and leaves its surviving inmates broken-hearted. This delusion grows until it becomes the instrument of repulsion and the justification of contempt. Men no longer warm themselves at the same fire, nor drink from the same stream. Ingenious fancy transfigures the familiar into the rare by her touch, into the coarse and forbidding by the contrast of her absence. The mind catches the temper of its haughty surroundings, and deems that it has the right to dazzle, because it has the power to enlighten.

The interior of the Palace illustrates the objects which the inmate reserves for her own contemplation. The range of corridors, "overvaulting grateful gloom," that connects the several apartments may mean the habitual circumspection which guards the judgment from being dissipated by the glare of unshadowed day. The fine touch, the nice discrimination superstitiously avoids too much contact with average estimates. Various moods of mind are represented by ideal landscapes. One, a morning scene, full of animal vigour, in which the clear air is resonant with the blast of the hunter's horn, buoys the imagination with the turbulent gladness of youth. From this we suddenly pass to another, in which, on a sandy tract by the glimmering light of a low large moon, "some one" paces for ever. We never see a mourner without asking, "Why does he weep?" Here the poet has accumulated all the vague images that intensify the essential mystery of sorrow. Then we behold the sea writhing in convulsive struggle with a threatening cliff; and, as we enter into the spirit of the contest, the scene changes, and an endless plain, a quiet river, peaceful herds, and a remote prospect, just relieved from sameness by a ragged thundercloud, dissolves the soul into the mingled prescience of its distant hope. A busy harvest scene, balanced by windy uplands, tells of autumnal plenty, and brings earth and her children into grateful relations; and immediately after a foreground of barren slag and cinder leads the eye backward to haughty crags that rise above the clouds, and volcanic fires reddening above the region of snow. From those occasional moods the soul fitly returns to its settled state, represented by an English home where tragic mystery is unknown, the struggle of life unfelt, the distant hope brought near, orderly, undisturbed, tree-embowered, and softened by the tender joy of evening.

All those mental conditions are or may be merely reflective. The sentiment or affection that they arouse is transfused or idly subsides. Strife and peace, joy and sorrow, hope and possession, are fields where the vagrant fancy amuses itself with variety. The lights and shadows of nature and the vicissitudes of man's lot are most fertile in their extreme degrees to the searcher for indolent pleasure. The external world will echo back to us in the mood in which we question it. If we ask for repetition of a sound, it will reverberate a sound. If we ask for wisdom, it will re-echo wisdom. Neither heaven nor earth is lifeless. The clouds are more than masses of vapour. We may not believe in Oreads or Naiads, but still the mountain and the ocean are beings to us; they are instinct with our life and wise with our experience. They sleep and wake, smile and frown, as we do. Calm answers to calm, tear to tear, storm to storm, desolation to desolation. Deep cries aloud to deep. It is not without a meaning that God calls on man to reason with Him in the audience of the mountains. The vast, the steadfast, the enduring, the unconquerable, are lessons for the heart and not luxury for the eye. They preside over the genesis of heroism. They are not to be plucked and flung away like blossoms that would never bear fruit.

After the moods connected with local scenery come those suggested by historic actions and incidents. Saviour, martyr, enthusiast, patriot, myth, legend, and superstition, all smoothed and rounded by the flow of ceaseless ages, all blanched and bleached by the winds and rains of centuries, all reduced by familiar adaptation by the use of a thousand hands, all etherealized by passing through a thousand poetic moods, all gathered in from the shores of time as relics and mementoes of wrecks in which the loftiest efforts of man foundered and sank, are stored in the museum of the beauty-loving mind. It was not for this that God set His chosen ones to aspire, to dare, to suffer. There never was a wrong done on earth for which there was not a counterpoise and a remedy in fore-ordained and calculated indignation at wrong. But this indignation was not meant to be the sheet lightning of an imperturbable mood. The lives of heroes were not crushed by the heel of oppression that they might yield a sweeter perfume for future generations of patrons of art. The world is something better than a gladiatorial show to which heaven sends combatants for the amusement of the cultured masters of mankind. The maid-mother did not mourn to immortalize the wives and mistresses of painters, and to impart a fresh grace to the beautiful. The hope of a kingdom of heaven did not rise and perish that supercilious and unsympathizing refinement might gather flowers on its tomb. It is no desecration that Christ should inspire the painter's pencil or the poet's pen or the sculptor's chisel; it is no desecration that His Name should be associated with our grandest musical compositions; but it would be a desecration if Christ, the people's long-expected Ideal answering to the design of heaven, whom the people accepted, whom the select and refined rulers slew, and whom the people raised from the dead, that is, to whose actual resurrection they by their faith gave historic reality and fame—it would be a desecration if this Christ were made the inspiration of an art that should never be a solace to the people, and which should only lull the gifted and the privileged into forgetfulness of the people's wants and the people's wrongs. Who are entitled to whatever of soothing power the poetic conception of Redeemer, martyr, saint, or sage can yield, if not those who bore them for a better end? Have they forfeited their claim to the chastening recollections because they have been robbed of the solid good which their heroes died to achieve? It was their affection that gave life to the legend. It was their undying trust in their own destiny that immortalized the sons who strove for them. To them belongs the substantial good, to them belongs the civilizing influence.

But unloving culture, appropriating all the hopes that popular instinct in its period of baffled endeavour had bequeathed for the consolation of happier days, wreathes them into a thing of beauty for the artistic soul, and sums up the injustice by shaping the forsaken struggles of the despoiled people into a mosaic. Having lined the Palace walls with landscapes, pictured legends, and portraits of bards, having ceiled it with the sheltering ministry of angels, there remains as a pavement—mankind. Having torn all the gold from the granite in whose tortured womb it had been purified through primeval fires, the granite itself is put to baser use. Having wrung the precious attar from the bruised and bleeding flowers, the rifled mass is flung underfoot.

> Below was all mosaic choicely plann'd
>   With cycles of the human tale
> Of this wide world, the times of every land
>   So wrought, they will not fail.
>
> The people here, a beast of burden slow,
>   Toil'd onward, prick'd with goads and stings ;
> Here play'd, a tiger, rolling to and fro
>   The heads and crowns of kings ;
>
> Here rose, an athlete, strong to break or bind
>   All force in bonds that might endure,
> And here once more like some sick man declined,
>   And trusted any cure.
>
> But over these she trod :
>
> . . . .

We have to remind ourselves from time to time that the Palace is a mental condition, an intellectual habit, a system of abstract beauty. There is an external material building, modelled on the inner idea ; but we must occasionally, to follow the poet's meaning, distinguish the two, and conceive the Palace of Art to be the educated, enriched, and arranged consciousness of an individual soul. When the soul, then, is said to be solitary, it is not implied that she is alone by separation from companions, but alone in unsympathetic selfishness and in alienation from the interests of mankind. She is in the midst of friends and admirers who hang upon her accents, but she owns no common purpose with them.

> And those great bells
> Began to chime. She took her throne:
> She sat betwixt the shining Oriels,
> To sing her songs alone.

The description that follows reminds us of some brilliant festive scene where the resources of opulence and of intellect reflect and intensify each other, and some inspired master of conversation pours from the exhaustless treasure-house of his memory the conquered spoils of every science to a rapt circle of listeners. The kings of every region of literature adorn his triumphal procession. Fed by tributaries from the whole domain of nature, a mighty stream of thought, lit by gorgeous imagery, pours its endless tide.

> And thro' the topmost Oriels' coloured flame
> Two godlike faces gazed below;
> Plato the wise, and large-brow'd Verulam,
> The first of those who know.

And all those names, that in their motion were
  Full-welling fountain-heads of change,
Betwixt the slender shafts were blazon'd fair
  In diverse raiment strange :

Thro' which the lights, rose, amber, emerald, blue,
  Flush'd in her temples and her eyes,
And from her lips, as morn from Memnon, drew
  Rivers of melodies.

Teeming mines of mental wealth, perfect mastery of copious expression, the physical soundness that gives an equipoise to our twofold nature and ensures an easy control over every faculty, a swift obedience from the whole battalioned artillery of illustration and proof, the steadying consciousness of power, the warming rush of the successful onslaught, delighted admiration in the gaze, murmured applause on the lips of each listener, every appliance of luxury that can stimulate the spirit, every victory of cunning contrivance that can extend the region and multiply the objects of sense, all the majesty of strength, all the achieved sovereignty over willing minds, is squandered on an idle intellectual display.

No nightingale delighteth to prolong
  Her low preamble all alone,
More than my soul to hear her echo'd song
  Throb thro' the ribbed stone ;

> Singing and murmuring in her feastful mirth,
> Joying to feel herself alive,
> Lord over nature, Lord of the visible earth,
> Lord of the senses five ;
>
> Communing with herself : "All these are mine,
> And let the world have peace or wars,
> 'Tis one to me."

The lights are lit in wreaths and anadems and hollowed moons of precious stone to bewilder the imagination into oblivion of earth by their mimicry of the skies, and wise and great are raised to the rank of gods that their sole living compeer may reign alone in unapproached supremacy. From this delirious height of flattered pride, this solitary throne of unsocial and recoiling sensitiveness, the ordinary joys of men seem grossness, and their efforts towards better things a hopeless frenzy of self-destruction.

> O God-like isolation which art mine,
> I can but count thee perfect gain,
> What time I watch the darkening droves of swine
> That range on yonder plain.
>
> In filthy sloughs they roll a prurient skin,
> They graze and wallow, breed and sleep ;
> And oft some brainless devil enters in,
> And drives them to the deep.

The old Pharisaic monopoly in law and religion is repeated in philosophy and art. Every article of knowledge that can be used as a key to the kingdom of right and truth, natural science, the moral instinct, the resurrection of the dead, is possessed, save the master-key. The master-key is the one further acquisition of knowledge—the sheath, and bond, and crown of all knowledge; that knowledge is the heaven-chartered right of all men. The master-key is love, not of God, which may be a selfish love, but of those whom God loves—men. The master-key is faith, not faith in Christ, which may be a selfish faith, but faith in what Christ did to establish the dignity and the destiny of man. Whether a man believes in one God or a thousand gods, whether he believes in Christ or Mahomet, unless he believes in the unbounded progress of man on earth he is an antitheist and an antichrist, for he refuses and resists the purpose and the will of God. Though I understand all mysteries and all knowledge, and though I have all faith so that I could remove mountains, and have not love, I am nothing; and though I bestow all my goods to feed the poor, and though I give my body to be burned, and have not love, it profiteth me nothing. All knowledge is nothing unless it is conditional, and accompanied by the consciousness that it is the birthright of man in every state, and rank, and clime. All help to man profits nothing if it be done to gain the quick harvest of thanks, and is not directed to the regeneration of races. Faith, hope, and love are one in essence and in object. Faith is loving hope, hope is trusting love, and love is hopeful trust in the sufficiency of virtue and the equal distribution of the highest happiness. The absence of this love is characteristic of the gifted and the privileged. They will not open the kingdom to others, and they cannot constitute a kingdom in themselves.

A consideration of wide importance now demands settlement. The Poet decides it, but sufficient attention may not be given to his determination. No doubt can exist as to the possible relative value of a pure and largely-endowed mind. But a further question arises: What is the likelihood that such a mind, accustomed to hold itself aloof in haughty isolation from the common herd, and to display its brilliancy to a chosen circle of admirers, will learn that it is a steward and not an owner? In what direction will it develop? What is its moral standing ground? A soul, educated and refined just so far as to see the beautiful and shrink from the coarse and ungraceful around it, capacious to receive and mighty to execute, with wealth of garnered grain and hand of skilful strength to scatter, yet spurning the fallows that hunger to produce, and hoarding its heaps in granaries kept for show, is a devil needing only one step of additional progress to become a god. In contrasting good with evil we must not confound imperfect degrees of good with positive evil, and so in reality contrast good with good. Imperfect degrees of good, the nearer they approach to perfect good by what they possess, the nearer they seem to approach to perfect evil by what they want. A being with all the attributes of God, save the will to communicate happiness, would differ from God in the absence of love, and from a demon in the absence of active hate. A movement on either side would consummate good or evil. On which side is it most probable that the movement will be made? We might imagine that the tendencies were equal. Some would argue that the evil tendency is the strongest, if not irresistible. Let it be remembered that the apparent twofold capacity has not been reached by two distinct processes of evil and good, but by one process of good. There was no necessary step towards hate in the whole progress that led to intellectual sovereignty. The very habit of isolation, the sensitive recoil from the mean and commonplace, and the consequent severance from the multitude, was an essential part of the struggle to a higher and purer level of thought. He who would raise men must unlearn and avoid their customs, and he can do this only by shunning contagious intercourse with them. To cast off this mechanically-acquired disdain is a final achievement, without which all that went before would be in vain; but we must not class the man who stops short at it with the sensual and malignant. We must not mistake the absence of the highest good for the presence of the highest evil. We are prone to do so because the sight of great powers unused for good strikes us as monstrous. As the animal form approaches the human, it is never so deformed as at the last stage. As man approximates to the godlike, the deficiencies that, associated with positive and vulgar vice, would pass unnoticed, emerge into glowing conspicuousness. We do not wonder at want of love in a gross and sensual nature; it shocks us in the pure and cultured. So the elder son in the parable is to the indiscriminate eye more morally guilty than his profligate brother. But, in fact, while the one has a past life to retrace, and a new nature to remould, the other requires only a single advance to make in order to become perfect as his father.

Art without love is stunted, maimed, abortive, but it is on the verge of symmetry. The tongues of angels without love are a tinkling cymbal, but with it they are the harmony of heaven. Self-sacrifice without love profits not, but with love it sits on the throne of God. In our resentment at the sight of power wanting love, we forget that the vanity of vanities is love wanting power.

But the distinction which is now insisted on is that between imperfect good and positive evil. It has been intimated that Tennyson pronounces a judgment relative to this distinction. He does so by implication in the concluding portion of the poem; but his meaning will be more intelligible by adverting for a few moments to his "Vision of Sin." There the course and result of positive evil are described. A youth with an aspiring soul, crushed down to earth by the weight of his baser nature, enters a palace, where a company of revellers, jaded with their last debauch, are languidly waiting till with recruited vigour they can renew their orgies. In the interval of sensual enjoyment they are utterly resourceless. No device of art is at hand to minister to a cultured taste, or to beguile them to a higher tract of thought. Nothing is seen but "heaps of gourds, and skins of wine, and piles of grapes." Their mode of life is pictured by the wild excitement and voluptuous movements of a dance. But each morning from the uplands, God, in the symbol of sunrise, offers the awful gift of a better life, and each day, and month, and year there floats from the same region satiety and leanness of soul, and the final loss of all nobleness, as the alternative of refusal. The heavy vapour of moral death envelops the palace, and the result is seen in the "gray and gap-tooth'd man," who with vindictive remorse rails at virtue, liberty, and heaven. The "winged horse" that the heavy rider repressed in early days is now a starved and broken-winded "brute." Nothing remains but "maudlin gall" and bitter "mockeries of the world." The vision finally shifts, and again the mountain range appears, but where the palace stood are "men and horses pierced with worms," bodies and souls reduced to a common level, and sharing a common fate. A voice asks, "Is there any hope?" and an answer peals back in a language that none can understand.

If we compare those two souls,—that in the "Palace of Art" exulting in godlike isolation, and that in the "Vision of Sin" immersed in sense and perishing with the natural decay of sense,—we cannot, apart from the poet's award, have any hesitation in assigning to them their fitting places in the moral scale. But while we despair for the one we are indignant with the other. Our despair is in reference to the possibility of personal redemption. Our indignation is in reference to the amount of possible good to others that is left unaccomplished. The single flaw in the æsthetic soul is exasperating; and since exasperation is a more vehement emotion than hopelessness, we assume that they who provoke it are the greatest offenders. And then we take the words of Christ concerning publicans and sinners, who were the social outcasts, the poor and the ignorant, by whose enforced degradation Pharisaic respectability maintained itself in Jerusalem, and we apply them to the wealthy sensualist who never awakes from the leaden lethargy of self-indulgence.

The comparison lies between the soul of the lover of art, beauty, and culture, who is not yet a lover of men, and the soul of him who is devoted to animal gratification; and the question is, which of the two is likeliest to feel the sting of discontent, and to aspire to a yet unattained good. A slave of old was placed in the triumphal car, to remind the victorious general as he rode through the acclaiming city that he was mortal.

God Himself reminds men in their intellectual triumph that they are human. It is only a truism to say that in proportion as our views widen, as our knowledge grows more clear, as our judgment becomes more just, the wider will our sympathies extend ; for it is only saying that the more we rise above the brute, the more attractive and diffusive must our humanity be. The most sordid joys are most exclusively guarded. The privileges that maintain these joys are always most desperately defended. The growth of society is from exclusive power to universal knowledge. Unjust political privileges, so far as the consciences of their possessors are concerned, will be retained for ever. It is when the political monopoly produces learning and refinement that the vessel overflows. The rights of men were never explicitly stated until at that period before the French Revolution when increasing enlightenment and civilization were pent within the bonds of an iron despotism. The soul becomes more tender and more just in proportion as its horizon enlarges. The bud may have to struggle hard against the environment that once protected it before it can burst into verdure ; the moth must strain its formless shell before it expands into summer beauty, yet none the less when its hour has come the final transformation cannot be delayed. The soul may find it difficult to overcome the habits of fastidious seclusion which sheltered it from the encroachments of the vicious and the mean, but the "riddle of the painful earth" will flash through it with ever more vivid intensity as the growing light of knowledge contrasts with the surrounding darkness. As the appliances that heal and strengthen are ascertained and proved, so do the wounds and bruises of our race become more distinct. The spirit delivered from the rule of its earthly companion may eddy for a time round a centre of its own, but it will soon yield to kindred attractions and blend with the human tide.

The danger of science is that it accustoms us to look at our earth not as the abode of mingled light and shade, joy and sorrow, but as a planet shining with unbroken, because distant, planetary light. This danger is soon lost in the throes of an unappeasable home-sickness. The still music of humanity becomes more attractive than the music of the spheres. The exquisite sense that retired in pain for a season from the sight of moral and material deformity returns for ever to relieve and to redress. The abysmal deeps of personality, swept and garnished by art, will entertain no demons. God inspires a divine despair and a righteous self-scorn. Shadows of the actual world, sorrows and horrors of real life, loathsome, amorphous, unnatural, which the eye only glanced at and turned away in disgust, haunt the imagination. The unity of law, the reality of progress, the undisguisable fact that mankind are not toiling in a slavish circle, but going ever onward in an uninterrupted march, startles the spectator to the discovery that if he lingers to gaze he will be left behind.

> A spot of dull stagnation, without light
> Or power of movement, seem'd my soul,
> 'Mid onward-sloping motions infinite
> Making for one sure goal.
>
> A still salt pool, lock'd in with bars of sand,
> Left on the shore; that hears all night
> The plunging seas draw backward from the land
> Their moon-led waters white.
>
> A star that with the choral starry dance
> Join'd not, but stood, and standing saw
> The hollow orb of moving Circumstance
> Roll'd round by one fix'd law.

In the biography of a soul Tennyson has given us the history of society under refining and humanizing influences. Neither an individual soul nor a section of society can clothe itself in light and refuse to shine on the world. Any attempt to do so will fail. Life is not a pageant to be gazed upon. Nature does not pose itself for the artist. Motion, life, growth, are indispensable to every true work of art. If it has not the life of nature it will not live. To feel this universal life, to be a part of it, to be conscious of it, to help its pulses to beat more fully, to add to the current of its progress, to lose ourselves and our interests in the sublime mystery of self-evolving destiny, is love. To be without love is death. It is to "moulder with the dull earth's mouldering sod." While this mingling with corruption is unfelt by the sensualist, it is torture, terror, and shame to the whetted sensibilities of the soul that has fed on the beautiful.

As the sympathies quicken and duty is recognised, the first sounds of human fellowship are distant and strange. A new land, a new sphere of action, a new and greater faculty is discovered. But it seems too late. "I have found a new land, but I die." The soul is only passing through a stage of advance. The goal of self-sacrifice is gained. The royal robe is cast aside. The Palace is forsaken for a cottage. The soul loathes its secret joy, and retires that it may perfect itself in love. There is none of the jealous Puritanism that malignantly denies to others the pleasures it cannot appreciate; there is none of the despair of the wearied and sated voluptuary who pronounces the world to be vexation of spirit because he has wasted his powers and misspent his life. Let the beautiful Palace remain, that it may be open to all.

> Yet pull not down my palace towers, that are
> So lightly, beautifully built:
> Perchance I may return *with others* there
> When I have purged my guilt.

THE PROMETHEUS VINCTUS.

THE vague sense of wonder and mystery which some poetic representations produce may arise from mere bewilderment of the understanding. We should always give the poet credit for having some better end in view. We should also assume that he is sufficiently master of his art to know that man's highest intelligence is the seat of true sublimity, and that the mind reaches a loftier mood when it fully takes in and comprehends a definite object than when its vision is impeded by encompassing mist and imagination usurps the place of reason. The giant form of the Eastern legend that grew on the eye of the astonished fisherman out of the cloud was more awful to behold than the shapeless vapour that filled the space between earth and heaven. A great generalization is more sublime than the confusion of facts which it reduces to order. We may hope that our admiration for the "Prometheus Vinctus" would not be lessened if it flowed no longer from the region and the quality of the unknown. And it is also to be assumed that we may safely confine ourselves to the precise materials which the artist has provided for his special purpose. Out of an unlimited and heterogeneous mass of myth and legend he has taken a few clearly defined characters for the construction of his drama. The distinct relations in which those characters stand to each other, as he has arranged them, would be destroyed if we confused and encumbered our memories with all the fables of Greek mythology that have a nominal association with the subject. The characters of Zeus and Prometheus, as they are here presented to us, are the subject on which we are to form a judgment, and not these characters as described in the works of other writers or in other writings of Æschylus.

The tragedy commences with a spectacle that arrests and fixes our sympathies. Strength and Force, two rugged giants representing the might of Zeus, compel Vulcan, the representative of mechanical skill, to fasten Prometheus to a savage rock overhanging the ocean. Vulcan shudders over his task, and bewails the necessity under which he works; but his brutal masters threaten him with a similar fate if he resists or shows unwillingness. A deed of merciless torture is minutely described. The limbs of the prisoner are riveted to the cliff. An iron wedge is driven through his chest. Chains are strung around his ribs till not a muscle can writhe. He endures without a murmur or a struggle. The executioners depart with mocking insults, leaving him to be scorched by the glaring sun, with no possibility of rest, or change of posture, or intermission of agony. Then he addresses himself to the powers of inanimate nature—

> Calm ether, winds whose nimble pinion quivers,
> Cool gurgling founts that swell to mighty rivers,
> And multitudinous dimple of the sea,
> And earth, of all the mother, and of me,
> And circled sun beholding all things fair,
> Behold what wrongs a god from gods I bear!
> See crushed with what pains,
> Till millenniums have flown,
> In dishonouring chains,
> I must struggle alone:
> For a new monarch reigns
> With the blest near his throne.
> Woe! woe! through an eternity of woe
> The present throbs into the coming throe,
> And endless night reveals no morning glow.
> And yet what say I? All things yet to be
> Belonging to my chosen part I see.
> I calculate my sorrows ere they rise;
> No unexpected loss can bring surprise.
> He who foreknowing treads the path that fate
> Bestrews with shivered hopes and burning hate,

Should bear in silence—though to tell the pain,
Silence and words strive equally in vain.
I succoured mortals—this my one offence,
Those chains and tortures are the consequence.
The stolen spark of fire to earth I bring,
Of arts the teacher, and of joys the spring,
This deed and these intentions I repay,
Nailed to a rock, of sun and storms the prey.
(88-113.)

Strength, on the first appearance on the stage, had explained, in words that would not sound amiss from a modern cynic, that their object in punishing Prometheus was that he—

Jove's sovereign power alone to serve might learn,
And cease to show a philanthropic turn. (10, 11.)

Or, as the lines might be rendered—

Might learn that fear of God is wisdom's plan,
Not dulled or weakened by the love of man.

This attempt to improve the lot of mortals was an interference with an opposite purpose of Zeus, as we are afterwards informed. The Ocean nymphs come to Prometheus, in answer to his cry, and lament the lawlessness of Zeus. He assures them that the time will come when circumstances will be wholly altered ; when Zeus will eagerly seek his aid, and when that aid will be gladly given. He further explains, at their request, the events that terminated in his present disaster. A war had broken out in heaven among the gods, some seeking to effect a revolution, and to raise Zeus to the throne of Saturn; others striving to maintain the established order. Prometheus (who throughout the play is characteristically the advocate of counsel in antagonism to brute force) knew that the victory would be won by whichever side employed the devices of policy and prudence. He first addressed himself to the Titans, and advised them to adopt the means that alone could succeed. They scornfully rejected his proposal, and preferred to conquer by strength. Prometheus, though (being a Titan himself) he would have wished that the victory should be with his kindred, yet choosing above all else that he who used policy rather than prudence should win the victory, next made overtures to Zeus, who accepted his offer, and, by his aid, overthrew his adversaries. The new monarch, in arranging his kingdom, took no account of men, or rather was planning to extirpate the race utterly, and introduce some new creation. Prometheus alone took their part, and frustrated the intentions of Zeus, by conveying fire from heaven to them. Pitying their miserable condition and abject fears of death, he gave them the bright vision of hope to flit between them and the grave, and engaged their thoughts with projects of varied improvement.

The ills of man you've heard : I formed his mind,
And through the cloud of barb'rous ignorance
Diffused the beams of knowledge. I will speak,
Not taxing them with blame, but my own gifts
Displaying, and benevolence to them.
They saw indeed, they heard ; but what availed
Or sight, or sense of hearing, all things rolling
Like the unreal imagery of dreams,
In wild confusion mixed ? The lightsome wall
Of finer masonry, the raftered roof
They knew not ; but, like ants, still buried, delved
Deep in the earth, and scooped their sunless caves.
Unmarked the seasons changed, the biting winter,
The flower perfumed spring, the ripening summer
Fertile of fruits. At random all their works,
Till I instructed them to mark the stars,
Their rising, and, a harder science yet,
Their setting. The rich train of marshalled numbers
I taught them, and meet array of letters.
T' impress these precepts on their hearts I sent
Memory, the active mother of all wisdom.
I taught the patient steer to bear the yoke,
In all his toils joint-labourer with man.
By me the harnessed steed was trained to whirl
The rapid car, and grace the pride of wealth.
The tall barque, lightly bounding o'er the waves,
I taught its course, and winged its flying sail.
To man I gave these arts : with all my wisdom
Yet want I now one art, that useful art
To free myself from these afflicting chains.

(450-480.) POTTER.

Io, the victim of the love of Zeus and the jealousy of Juno, comes on the scene and relates her miserable story. Prometheus informs her that eventually Zeus will seek to engage in an amour which will be the cause of his dethronement if persisted in, inasmuch as the object of his love was destined to bear a son who would prove greater than his father. This secret of fate was known to Prometheus only, and he declares that he will never reveal it until after he has been delivered from his bonds, which deliverance was to be accomplished against the will of Zeus by Eracles, a descendant of Io. After the departure of Io the Oceanides protest against the loves of the great with the lowly, and lament the lot of those whom Zeus compels to his embrace. Prometheus answers that the licentious desires of Zeus will yet work his ruin.

Yet Zeus, albeit most absolute of will,
Shall turn to meekness,—such a marriage-rite
He holds in preparation, which anon
Shall thrust him headlong from his gerent seat
Adown the abysmal void, and so the curse
His father Chronos muttered in his fall,
As he fell from his ancient throne and cursed,
Shall be accomplished wholly. No escape
From all that ruin shall the filial Zeus
Find granted to him from any of his gods,
Unless I teach him. I the refuge know,

And I, the means. Now, therefore, let him sit
And brave the imminent doom, and fix his faith
On his supernal noises, hurtling on
With restless hand the bolt that breathes out fire ;
For these things shall not help him, none of them,
Nor hinder his perdition when he falls
To shame, and lower than patience : such a foe
He doth himself prepare against himself,
A wonder of unconquerable hate,
An organizer of sublimer fire
Than glares in lightnings, and of grander sound
Than aught the thunder rolls, out thundering it,
With power to shatter in Poseidon's fist
The trident-spear which, while it plagues the sea,
Doth shake the shores around it. Ay, and Zeus,
Precipitated thus, shall learn at length
The difference betwixt rule and servitude.

(943-963.) MRS. BROWNING.

Hermes now appears, bearing a command from Zeus that Prometheus should at once clearly explain what the nuptials were by means of which he was destined to lose the sovereignty of heaven, and threatening that if he refused to answer he should be cast down to Tartarus, whence after a long space of time he would be brought back to his former position to suffer as before, with the addition of a winged hound of Zeus—an eagle—perpetually rending his body and feeding on his liver. Prometheus replies with defiant scorn. The Oceanides, though they beseech him to relent and bend to necessity, yet, rather than desert him, prefer to share his fate. The play concludes with the description by Prometheus of the approaching storm of divine wrath.

> Truly bursts the doom on me!
> Earth is heaving like the sea,
> And the thunder bellows by;
> And the lightning's fiery curls
> Stream in clusters from the sky;
> And the whirlwind in its whirls
> Sweeps the dust up; and the blast
> Of every wind is hurrying fast
> With the rush of wild commotion,
> Leaping each against his brother,
> Mad to trample one another;
> And the sky is mixt with ocean,
> In confusion reconciled:
> Such a blast, with terror piled,
> 'Gainst me wings its rapid path,
> Sent from Zeus to do his wrath,
> Oh my dread mother! oh thou firmament,
> Rolling the common light of all, thou seest
> What violent harms I most unjustly suffer.
>
> (1116-1129.)
>
> Mr. Chapman: *Blackwood's Magazine*, xl. 740.

The impression left on our minds by the perusal of this tragedy is one of intense and lofty admiration for the divine hero who persists in protecting the weak and helpless race of men from the hate of a merciless tyrant by his own suffering. It would appear that his patronage was able to baffle the might of Zeus, and that all the tortures imposed on him were chiefly intended to force him to resign his guardianship and abandon men to destruction. He maintains his ground with unflinching resolution, and presents the grandest instance of devotion to duty that the mind can conceive. It need never have occurred to us that the poet had any other aim than this. Freedom, confronting and daring tyranny, was assuredly a subject worthy of and befitting the genius of Greece. It satisfied the contemporaries of Æschylus. It fails, however, to satisfy our more scrupulous age. The chief obstacle, it is said, to the satisfactory interpretation of the play arises from the difficulty of understanding how Prometheus was guilty and Zeus justified. No work was ever written that would not present an insuperable difficulty to its comprehension if we started with the assumption that it does not mean what it says, but something quite opposite. Why should we conclude that, notwithstanding his magnanimous innocence, Prometheus was guilty? Why should we settle in our minds that Zeus must be justified in spite of his manifest injustice and tyranny? The reason seems to be that Zeus is a god and Prometheus a man, and that a god by his nature must be right. Müller states it thus: "Tragedy," he says, "could not consist in a conflict between the free will of man and omnipotent fate." But Prometheus is not a man, nor is Zeus either omnipotent himself nor has he omnipotent fate on his side. The implied imputation of blasphemy or profanity is quite inadmissible. We can join equally in the protests and defiances of Prometheus or the delegated insults and threats of Zeus without exposing ourselves to the charge of formal impiety. Prometheus is a god as well as Zeus. We are reminded of this with a frequency that is suggestive of a purpose: while the early parts of the play in which the passages occur give them the force of a premise to an intended conclusion.

Vulcan (in lines 14, 15) says:

> But I am out of heart a kindred god
> To bind perforce to this storm-beaten cleft.

Again (line 29):

> A god, thou didst not fear the wrath of gods.

Strength, addressing Vulcan, makes the same admission (line 37):

> A god, god-hated, dost thou not abhor?

Prometheus himself founds his claim to

sympathy from the powers of nature on his being a god (line 92):

Behold what things a god from gods I suffer.

Again, he says to the approaching Oceanides:

Look on me prisoned, an ill-fortuned god.

The conflict, then, is not between god and man, but between a god of power and a god of love; and, in its first stage, the god of love is crushed and disgraced. But Zeus is not omnipotent, and his triumph is to be short-lived. Prometheus holds the key of destiny in his hands, and it is admitted that the doom of the dynasty of Zeus hangs on his consent or refusal to unlock the mystery. The Oceanides are said to give their verdict against Prometheus because during his conference with Hermes (line 972) they say:

They who reverence Nemesis are wise.

The critics to whom I am now referring give as the meaning of this line that "they only are sane and righteous who bow to necessity and accept the law of their superiors." This is simply a very serious mistranslation. They are "wise," the text says, who reverence Adrasteia or Nemesis. But there is a higher and a lower wisdom as there is a higher and a lower Nemesis. Prometheus, the far-seeing one, sees the higher wisdom and the higher Nemesis, and Zeus, the blind tyrant, sees only the lower. The tender, sympathetic Ocean nymphs, shocked at the appalling threats of divine fury hurled by Hermes at their favourite, beseech him in their momentary terror to yield, and save himself. The wisdom they refer to is the wisdom of self-preservation. The meaning of this counsel was that to escape the fury of Zeus he should surrender the human race to it. This would be only escaping an immediate and temporary Nemesis—the Nemesis that attends well-doing, and incurring the remote and eternal Nemesis—the Nemesis of evil-doing, which impended over Zeus, and would finally overwhelm in endless ruin him and all who abetted him in his arbitrary rule. It is Zeus, then, and not Prometheus, who acts unwisely as well as cruelly in striving against an inevitable fate. All the moral superiority is with the suffering Titan. "I know," he says in the commencement of the play, "that Zeus is harsh and makes right depend on his own will, but for all that he shall be hereafter softened in purpose when he shall be crushed as I am now: and, after quelling his ruthless rage, with eagerness, at some future day, shall he come into league and friendship with me that shall eagerly welcome his advances." (194—200.) He cannot submit to wrongful tyranny, though triumphant, but he declares his readiness to forgive the tyrant when his hour of destruction comes, though in the meantime he shall have endured all the pangs and tortures that vengeance can devise. On the other hand, Zeus, though he knows that his supremacy depends on the will of Prometheus, and that he must at last have to sue him for deliverance, cannot resort to conciliatory means, cannot bring himself to tolerate his victim, cannot refrain from savage insults and violence to the hated god who has resisted his self-asserted omnipotence. The Oceanides, though in their weak pity they would advise submission, prefer for themselves to descend to Tartarus with Prometheus rather than dwell on an earth governed by Zeus.

If the object of Æschylus were to enforce on his countrymen hatred of human tyrants by the description of a heavenly despot, an interpretation which Grote prefers to the forcible methods employed to bring the poet into harmony with modern religious ideas (vol. i., p. 37, note), and an interpretation which, though not the primary one, is certainly involved in it, it is obvious that the insistence on equality of godhead is readily transmissible to the human sphere.

> Behold what wrongs a man from men I suffer

implies as powerful an argument as when the proposition deals with the immortals. The rack and the throne contain men. The disputes of men, sovereigns, or serfs, are not of classes, or different orders of being, but of rights and wrongs.

The difficulty of the play, as we are now considering it, does not lie in itself, but in reconciling it with current beliefs. That is, the difficulty is not one of comprehension, but of acceptance. There is an obvious meaning, but we do not wish to admit it. Zeus is a tyrant, and it jars upon us to admit that a god can be a tyrant. Even after we have shown that Prometheus was a god also, and was therefore justifiable in his opposition, we, who are only mortal men, feel that we have no right to imitate him; and, if we cannot imitate, we dare not openly approve. Though the gods resist each other, men must look in silent reverence on a scene beyond their comprehension. But, though we cannot assume the rank of gods, and take our place in the war against Zeus, we can take the alternative method and deny—which was the real meaning of Æschylus—that Zeus was a god. Zeus was a god, and therefore could not possibly be in the wrong, is the argument of superstitious orthodoxy. The true argument is, Zeus was wrong, and therefore he could not be a god. This is the logic of Christianity. The greatest personage of the Hebrew race, and the father of all believers, laid it down as a fundamental axiom that the Being who rules the world is to be discerned by his possession of a quality which He created man capable of discerning. "Shall not the Judge of all the earth do right?" (Gen. xviii. 25). The office of universal ruler implies the indispensable presence of justice, and man is qualified to judge whether it is present or not. The being who has not justice, call him by what sacred name you may, is not ruler of all the earth. The greatest personage in the Christian Church refers to the same great rule as one of final and irreversible appeal. Replying to an imputation on God's righteousness, he says: This cannot be true, for, if it were, God would be unjust, and then, how could He judge the world? (Rom. iii. 6). We must not conceive an unjust God. Whatever is unjust is not God.

All through the drama there is an older order of things alluded to on which the rule of Zeus is an encroaching and irregular usurpation. The empire of Zeus is new and marked by the insolence of novelty. Vulcan says:

> The heart of Zeus is hard to be entreated,
> And every one is harsh who newly reigns. (34, 35.)

> Such ignominious chains
> This new king of the blest
> Invents for me. (95.)

> Know thyself and conform to measures new,
> For a new tyrant reigns among the gods. (317.)

> With him who newly fills the sovereign throne. (397.)

> Who else than I among these upstart gods
> Portioned to each his fit prerogative? (448.)

Prometheus is not a mouther of sedition. He represents the ancient system on which the arbitrary government of Zeus is explicitly said to be an unconstitutional innovation (156). According to the ancient order he is the friend and benefactor of man. The belief had become universal in the Pagan world that the gods were the enemies of mankind. If a man had a continued course of good fortune, his friends advised him to undergo some voluntary loss in order to appease the envy of the gods, who else would visit him with some terrible calamity. This idea was the parent of superstition. Men served the gods only from fear; and as fear is selfish, seeking personal safety only, and regards power and not moral qualities as the object of its services, the gods became monsters of vice, and their worshippers served them with sincere devotion. The man who would practise virtue must be an unbeliever in the popular deities. Prometheus is the restorer of the old order. In him the divine foresight, which is really the movable centre of omniscience, the wisdom gathered from the converging lines of the two eternities, is brought into lucid distinctness from the near-sighted prudence that sees in one direction only, and there only to the length of one's own shadow. When Strength has bound him to the rock, he addresses him with the brutal taunt:—

There now insult and robbing the immortals
Bestow their rights on creatures of a day.
Can dying men lighten thy freight of pains?
Falsely the gods miscall thee the Foreseer,
Thy very self hast need of a Foreseer
To loose the webs of Strength's superior art. (82-86.)

The rude minds of the instruments of despotism often catch the motives that inspire their employers and reflect them with the undisguised triumph of malevolence. The immortals despised men because they were mortal. Why should the sun shine for wretches creeping to their graves? This is the unspoken argument of the gods who dwelt on the clouds that exhaled from a suffering and struggling world. We are happy and the world of men is miserable, why should a drop from our cup of joy be lost on that arid sand?

Prometheus is the champion of wisdom against prudence, of counsel against strength, of love against hate, of justice against wrong, of religion against superstition, of the eternal against the temporal.

There are three distinct ideas of deity in the scheme of theology or divine government which Æschylus exhibits. There is the god of an arbitrary will delighting in men's agonies, ruling by force, controlling by fear, confining men to dark and joyless lives, because kindness begets happiness, and happiness rouses the buoyant spirit of independence. Zeus delights to reign over abject cowering slaves, whose souls never have a moment's respite from narrow care, whose bodily wants never leave the soul at liberty. In conformity with this policy of rule is his policy of repression. He crushes with bodily pains and tries to extinguish the soul's expansion by evaporating it in the fires of torture. Vulcan brings out the contrast:—

High-minded son of right-advising Themis,
I, indisposed to act as thou to suffer,
Must nail thy body to this savage peak,
Where never man nor voice of man shall come
To tell thee that thou sufferest not in vain. (18-20.)

Far away in the past of history, and in the soul's region of faith, there reigns a supreme God, the Creator of the universe, who is invisible save to Prometheus. He seems overthrown and uncrowned now because he meets force not by force, but by the silent action of a constructive principle. To this God, under the name of destiny or retribution, Prometheus appeals. He does not mean the blind destiny of tyrannic authority stamping its incoherent caprice on a pliant world, but the destiny of cause and corresponding consequence, of free action and fitting result, of tilth and produce, all controlled by justice and modified by mercy.

In depicting Zeus, Æschylus did not refer to the ruler of the gods, as his character was conceived by good and wise men. He described the popular Zeus, who personified human vices on a divine scale. There were two distinct cotemporaneous ideas of the same god. One was the god of the lower air vexed by storms; the other was the god of the empyrean, the calm, eternal wisdom that surrounds the universe and contains it, and is slowly reducing it to its own ordered peace. Both those gods were called Zeus. One was the god of tyrants, the torturer of men and defiler of women; the other was the Zeus of patriots and philosophers, the wise and silent distributor of justice, slow in operation because the result is to last for ever. It is to this Zeus that Prometheus appeals against his enemy. He does not appeal to him by name, because he is himself the true Zeus, entering into the struggle for the sake of man and enduring injustice. The persecuting Zeus is a usurper upheld by usurpers and men of crime and violence. The Titans failed to dethrone him, because they fought him with strength against strength and disdained the methods of wisdom.

Our experience in later ages is the same as that of former men. Power, modified it may be in some subtle way, but still power, rules. The crashing thunderbolt is forged by modern Vulcans into a thousand delicate instruments of torture or destruction. Save to the farseeing there is no trace of the fatherhood of God upon earth. The good are oppressed, the weak suffer, the toilers are unrecompensed. The cry of fear or anguish to heaven meets no response save in the hidden soul and in the promise of a future redemption. If we were to judge of the god that rules from the results of his government, we must conclude that he is the enemy of men. The best policy would be to recognise him practically in this character and worship him accordingly. To serve him by lofty deeds of virtue and love for men is the most certain way to provoke his hatred. It is best therefore to flatter and imitate him, to seek our own ease and happiness, and regard our fellow-men as he regards the whole race. To build gorgeous shrines to him, to elaborate and multiply ceremonies on the condition of receiving wealth from him to be used selfishly, and power to be employed after his model, is wise. It is, moreover, true religion; and anyone offering a different worship is profane and impious; and he should be made to suffer under the common hate of god and man. So might we speak now, and so might a Greek tragedian describe the popular creed of his day. It is the religion of prudence and expediency, and he who looks beyond what is expedient is certain to stumble against the actual.

The god we worship is a god of war, and we chant his praises as such. When nations go to war with each other they both sing *Te Deums* to the same god, and it is clearly understood that if either of them trusted to right, and acting on the principle that the battle is not to the strong, neglected to accumulate arms of destruction and to acquire skill in the use of them, god would desert the nation that trusted in righteousness and go over to the nation with strong battalions. No greater insult could be offered to this god than to seek to please him and win his favour by goodness or unselfishness. He would instantly join his true worshippers against such a man, and preside over them while they destroyed him. If, on the other hand, one were to assert that this god is a tyrant and a god of this world, and a friend of tyrants and men of this world—a god of pomp and show and the friend of men of pomp and show—a god who despises the poor, and the honest and sincere, and a friend of those who despise the poor and the honest and sincere—a god who abhors independence and love of truth, and the favourer of all who abhor independence and love of truth;—if one were to assert this, all the worshippers of this god would rise in indignation and pronounce him an atheist and unfit to inhabit the earth. It was prudent, therefore, of Æschylus to speak not in his own person, but to direct against itself the awe in which the mere name of God is held.

On the other hand, there is a God whom the

friendless, and the unfortunate, the weary and the heavy-laden, call upon; whom lovers of men, and teachers and liberators of men, invoke when they begin their labours, and look to with undimmed devotion from the darkness of their failure. He does not come to their relief; He does not open the prison door, nor stay the uplifted sword, nor extinguish the encircling flame. Yet in every age there have been men who, with strength and force and the executioner as their doom, cling to this God, and feel an unquenchable certainty that in good time He will deliver them. Would it not be an act of reverence towards this God of justice and love, if some Æschylus were to expose the false and unjust god as having no real existence, as being only a shadow projected from man's base nature on the walls of heaven and as obscuring from men's view the vision of its true Inhabitant?

It is argued that Zeus cannot be intended to appear as a tyrant by Æschylus, because in his other tragedies he depicts Zeus as the sovereign god of justice and goodness. This is only incontestable evidence that he had two distinct characters of Zeus in his mind, one true and one false.

Another mode of evading the conclusion to

which this play leads is the supposition that it is one of a trilogy, and that the concluding drama justifies the conduct of Zeus and shows Prometheus to have been in error. This is pure supposition. There is no ground for supposing that this play is not perfect in itself. We feel, moreover, that if the conduct of Zeus could be reconciled with justice, it can only be by an irreparable injury to justice. But there is no room for this supposition.

From the positions laid down in this drama any consistent conclusion arrived at must be in justification of Prometheus. He knew that Zeus would engage in an intrigue with a female destined to bear a son greater than his father. This is the knowledge which Zeus seeks from him and which he refuses to render. Here is the point in the contest which the tragedy leaves undecided. But it was known from current mythology that the decision must be in favour of Prometheus, and that his character must come forth loftier and purer, while Zeus must appear baffled and humiliated. Eracles slew the vulture or eagle that preyed on Prometheus, who then, returning good for evil, warned Zeus of his danger, as he had declared he would be ready to do. The story ends in the delivery of Prometheus and Thetis, the objects of the passions of Zeus, who is thus checked in his cruelty and his lust. Prometheus comes forth the far superior god.

But it could not have been the purpose of Æschylus to conclude the history while in fact its real matter was not concluded. The time had not come for Prometheus to triumph—nor has it come yet. There is a true and a false Jehovah, as there was a true and a false Zeus.

THE PROMETHEUS OF ÆSCHYLUS AND OF SHELLEY.

IN attempting to describe the relation which the "Prometheus Unbound" of Shelley bears to the "Prometheus Bound" of Æschylus we are impeded rather than expedited by the English poet's own declaration of his purpose. Æschylus exhibited the drama of human history in a contest between an unjust god, the hater of men, and a just god, the lover of men, in which the lover of men is vanquished and hurled to the nethermost hell, bearing with him the certain knowledge that in the inevitable development of events his doom must be reversed, and his victor and torturer changed into his suppliant and subject. This was the constitution of heavenly empire by which the condition of earth was explained and illustrated. Men were taught to struggle and to endure for the right, and to forget their sufferings, or to glory because of them in the thought that they were sharing the voluntary and mediatory sorrows of a righteous God. There was no longer adversity in defeat, nor humiliation in pain. The great and decisive moral victory of virtue over vice was made certain and brought nearer by each successive material victory of vice over virtue. The extent to which this representation has succeeded in producing, or preparing the way for, whatever amount of attained liberty or heroic motive exists in the world can scarcely be over-estimated. But manifestly until a time came when light and justice were so fixed, not only in human institutions, but in the universal soul of man, as that a return to superstition and tyranny was impossible, it was required imperatively that the story should remain unfinished. That Prometheus may do his work his bondage must continue. In later days the degree in which Christianity has proved a failure is mainly owing to the premature substitution of a triumphant for a crucified Christ. A perfectly unauthorized theory has been adopted that Æschylus wrote a second drama, in which Prometheus submits and is reconciled to Jupiter. This second drama, if it existed, would obliterate the first, and so far as the belief in its ever having existed prevails, it succeeds in so doing. Shelley wrote his "Prometheus Unbound" in rivalry to this imaginary "Prometheus Unbound" of Æschylus.

"He was averse," he says in his preface, "from a catastrophe so feeble as that of reconciling the champion with the oppressor of mankind. The moral interest of the fable, which is so powerfully sustained by the sufferings and endurance of Prometheus, would be annihilated if we could conceive of him as unsaying his high language and quailing before his successful and perfidious adversary." He might have rested content with the fact that if the supplementary drama had ever been written, it had disappeared in the struggle for immortality, and left the whole field to a survivor that more fitly expressed the nature, the wants, and the aspirations of man. Or he might have followed the direction indicated in the "Prometheus Bound," and produced a drama in which Jupiter is compelled to submit to Prometheus. "I know that Jupiter is harsh," the Prometheus of Æschylus says, "and makes justice depend on his own arbitrary will, but the time will come when, crushed as I am now, he will quell his rage and seek my friendship; and when that time comes I will gladly meet his advances." On the foundation, therefore, of the "Prometheus Bound," any sequel to it must have described Jupiter as submitting to Prometheus, and not Prometheus as submitting to Jupiter—evil as yielding to good, and not good to evil. But Shelley so much misconceived Æschylus, because of this imaginary drama, that he formally rejects him as a guide. "Should I live," he says, "to accomplish what I purpose, that is, produce a systematical history of what appear to me to be the genuine elements of human society, let not the advocates of injustice and superstition flatter themselves that I should take Æschylus rather than Plato as my model." But he had another immediate motive, which weighed more with him than any other, and would by itself have urged him to his task. He thought that the work of Prometheus was accomplished, and that the time for his deliverance was at hand. He wrote to hasten and help its advent. He believed that the description of the unbinding of Prometheus would affect the minds of men more powerfully than the picture of his sufferings. "The great writers of our own age," he says, "are, we have reason to suppose, the companions and forerunners of some unimagined change in our social condition, or the opinions which cement it. The cloud of mind is discharging its collected lightning, and the equilibrium between institutions and opinions is now restoring, or is about to be restored." Shelley unbound Prometheus to hasten and illustrate the unbinding of mankind. The feeling that

Prometheus ought not to have suffered at all was so strong with him that he exulted in obliterating at once the traces of the sorrow and of the tyranny that imposed it. But in this course he ran counter to human history and human nature.

Here we have one fundamental difference between Æschylus and Shelley. Æschylus wrote what he intended to be a complete and finished work. That fate seemed to hang suspended, and the superstructure of history was made to stand poised on a crisis, constituted its completeness. It arrested the eyes and touched the hearts of men, just because it was unfinished. It was morally complete because it was artistically incomplete. The only preparation for unbinding Prometheus would be by unbinding man: but the final unbinding of man depends on Prometheus being left bound. Shelley, in his eager passion, unbound Prometheus dramatically, in order that he might aid thus in loosening man's religious and political chains. But in precipitating the end he in reality destroyed the means. The true sequel to the drama of Æschylus is not the drama of a religious revolution, but an actual religious revolution. The design it has in view is the enthronement of a god of justice in men's hearts, instead of a god of tyranny and cruelty. This is carried out not by representing the god of justice as omnipotent and happy, but by representing him as vanquished, tortured, and reviled. Hatred of injustice is the strong wine under whose divine intoxication mankind have fought their greatest battles for freedom and light. Æschylus appeals to this principle. Prometheus was to be freed only in proportion as men made him their model while he hung on the rock. He became unbound by remaining bound. He was freed by men coming to his side and sharing his wrongs with him until no authorized doer of wrong existed on earth or was shadowed on heaven. Prometheus seeks deliverance for men, not for himself; and to deliver him before men were delivered would render all his endeavours and sufferings vain. He is represented as suffering that men may not be ashamed to suffer for the right. He continues impaled at the bidding of a tyrant, that earth may loathe tyrants and resist them, even at the risk and for the glory of being impaled with him. Shelley saw clearly enough that the submission and reconcilement of Prometheus to Jupiter would destroy all the Titan's power over mankind, and give the final victory to vice. If a throne were erected to him by the side of the throne of Jupiter, and if the proud rulers of the world honoured him and sacrificed to him, he would be the accomplice of Jupiter. This was what the asserters of the lost drama of Æschylus endeavoured to effect. Something like this has been done in the case of Christ. He came to dispost the bloodthirsty idol-god whom the degenerate Jews had put in the place of the just and merciful Jehovah. He came to bring healing to the broken-hearted, deliverance to the captive, liberty to the bruised. This could be done only by incurring the wrath and vengeance of the god of tyrants. But it was to be the work, not of a day, or an age, or a man; it was to be the work of successive ages, and successive lines of devoted men. To encourage men through all time to persist in doing this work, and knowing that the inevitable accompaniment of this work must be suffering and sorrow, He proposes Himself to the world as characteristically the sufferer and the man of sorrows. He consorted with the lost and the despised, and He raised the sharp outline of the Cross on every elevation to which his followers might aspire. But rich men took Him down from the Cross, and kings and princes soon patronized Him, and ruled in His name. This was what awoke Shelley's indignation, and drove him to attempt the overthrow of all religion, seeing that it was always made the buttress of unjust dominion. In liberating Prometheus, his intention was to set man free. But is his plan the right one? The object is to induce men to surrender somewhat to each other; to honour each other: to bear each other's burthens. How is this to be done? How are we to be taught to be heroes, not in the storm of the battle-field or the agony of the wreck only, but in the mart, and at the hearth, and in the social arena? Under what king shall we be able to conquer the terrors and seductions of earth by conquering self? Christ was put before the minds of the early Christians as emphatically Christ crucified. Just as emphatically and persistently is He now displayed as Christ glorified, enthroned, and triumphant. Which Christ produced the greatest effects on the minds of men—the Christ who was lifted on the cross and drew all men unto Him, or the Christ who has dignities and salaries to bestow? No doubt the later Christ produces a greater and wider effect, but it is in exact opposition to the work of the earlier Christ. Let us compare the last scene of the Prometheus of Æschylus with that of the Prometheus of Shelley.

In deed, and no longer in word, the earth reels, and the thunder bellows past us, and lightning flashes glare, and hurricane blasts whirl the dust, and winds battle with winds, and heaven struggles with the deep. All this, driving panic to my soul, descends on me from Jove. O, dread majesty of my mother earth! O, ether, that spreadest light, a common blessing! you see what wrongs I unjustly suffer.

Those are the words of the bound Prometheus as he is about to be cast into Tartarus. Shelley's Prometheus, after he has been delivered by Hercules, surveys the prospect that opens before him :—

> There is a cave,
> All overgrown with trailing odorous plants,
> Which curtain out the day with leaves and flowers,
> And paved with veinéd emerald, and a fountain
> Leaps in the midst with an awakening sound.
> . . . .
> And there is heard the ever-moving air,
> Whispering without from tree to tree, and birds,
> And bees ; and all around are mossy seats,
> And the rough walls are clothed with long soft grass ;
> A simple dwelling, which shall be our own ;
> Where we will sit and talk of time and change,
> As the world ebbs and flows, ourselves unchanged.
> . . . .
> And hither come, sped on the charméd winds, . . .
> The echoes of the human world, which tell
> Of the low voice of love, almost unheard,
> And dove-eyed pity's murmured pain, and music,
> Itself the echo of the heart, and all
> That tempers or improves man's life, now free.

This is a description of regenerated society. It is in keeping with the tenderness of Shelley's genius that he should substitute those soft scenes of pathetic home affection, as affording a greater stimulus to men pining for rest, than could be supplied by the sight of their tortured and defiant champion. The scene presents Shelley's idea of the end which Prometheus sought to gain for men by the sacrifice of himself. Shelley would gain this end merely by describing its charms, as if all that the world sought was equal happiness. He made the deep mistake, and it is strikingly characteristic of him, that the strongest passion of the soul is philanthropy. Prometheus represents man, Asia, love or beauty. The very picture of the happiness that follows their union will remove all need for suffering Titans in the future. So Shelley reasoned. He forgot that society is saved, not by the readiness of the multitude to be happy, but by the willingness of each man to surrender his propensity to monopolize happiness, and that this seemingly easy result requires the example of a god suffering for all, and inspiring a few to dare and endure for others in preference to enjoying for themselves. There is no return to innocence for the individual or the race. The golden age that is to come must come from the crucible. Long hence, if ever, shall we be able to change our Good Friday into a feast day.

The typical character of Shelley's Prometheus, the identification of the champion with the race, not only suggested to him the composition of the drama, but has affected every part of its structure. The Prometheus of Æschylus is a person distinct and isolated, suffering persecution at the hands of a personal tyrant. The whole occurrence is without us. We see one whose virtues we revere, whose sorrows we pity and resent. There is no taint of reflected self-interest in our compassion or our indignation. We feel for another, who suffers wrongfully, and we are disciplined to feel for all others who suffer wrongfully. The humanity of Shelley's Prometheus is so representatively depicted that his sorrows tend to beget in us that most demoralizing and emasculating of all emotions—self-pity. There is a plaintive self-consciousness in his lamentations that is signally absent from the proud utterances of the Titan of the Greek poem. Those lines in the opening address to Jupiter—

> The wingless, crawling hours, one among whom—
> As some dark Priest hales the reluctant victim—
> Shall drag thee, cruel King, to kiss the blood
> From these pale feet—

would never have been spoken by the Prometheus of Æschylus.

The sufferings of the hero of the Greek drama are physical. His bodily tortures are set before us almost obtrusively, at the very commencement of the tragedy, and we never forget to the end that one torn by pangs of nerve and sinew is speaking. In this way our sympathies are drawn out of us to their proper object. The sufferings of Shelley's Prometheus are mainly mental. Even when physical tortures are described, they are so mingled with elemental impersonations that our sense of compassion grows confused.

> The crawling glaciers pierce me with the spears
> Of their moon-freezing crystals ; the bright chains
> Eat with their burning cold into my bones.
> Heaven's wingéd hound, polluting from thy lips
> His beak in poison not his own, tears up
> My heart ; and shapeless sights come wandering by,
> The ghastly people of the realm of dream,
> Mocking me : and the Earthquake fiends are charged
> To wrench the rivets from my quivering wounds
> When the rocks split and close again behind :
> While from their loud abysses howling throng
> The genii of the storm, urging the rage
> Of whirlwind, and afflict me with keen hail.

When Mercury calls the furies to punish the refusal to render up the secret that affects Jupiter, we only read of passions and affections that exclude the idea of personality and disallow dramatic interest.

> We are ministers of pain and fear,
> And disappointment, and mistrust, and hate,
> And clinging crime ; and as lean dogs pursue
> Through wood and lake some struck and sobbing fawn,
> We track all things that weep, and bleed, and live,
> When the great King betrays them to our will.

. . . .

As from the rose which the pale priestess kneels
To gather for her festal crown of flowers
The aërial crimson falls, flushing her cheek,
So from our victim's destined agony
The shade which is our form invests us round,
Else we are shapeless as our mother Night.

Of the same character is the representation of the worse than failure of all previous efforts to set right the errors and crimes of societies:

Dost thou boast the clear knowledge thou waken'dst for
    man!
Then was kindled within him a thirst which outran
Those perishing waters; a thirst of fierce fever,
Hope, love, doubt, desire, which consume him for ever.

One came forth of gentle worth
Smiling on the sanguine earth:
His words outlived him, like swift poison
    Withering up truth, peace, and pity.
Look! where round the wide horizon
    Many a million-peopled city
Vomits smoke in the bright air.
Mark that outcry of despair!
'Tis his mild and gentle ghost
    Wailing for the faith he kindled.

. . . .

Remit the anguish of that lighted stare;
Close those wan lips: let that thorn-wounded brow
Stream not with blood; it mingles with thy tears!
Fix, fix those tortured orbs in peace and death,
So thy sick throes shake not that crucifix,
So those pale fingers play not with thy gore.

> O, horrible! thy name I will not speak,
> It hath become a curse.

Here, Prometheus is made to shrink from his own example, as reproduced in the person of Christ, and Christ is represented as horrified at the unforeseen result of His own teaching. It might be argued that the poet only described the shadow of a doubt crossing the soul of the sufferer in the crisis of his agony, were it not that the deliverance, which is the end of the process, must be taken as a practical commentary on the poet's estimate of suffering as the attribute of all efforts to save. Shelley considered that suffering was unnatural and unnecessary in a deliverer. He conceived that view from a misconception of Christianity; and his misconception throws some confusion over his management of the whole subject. Prometheus, as we read in the original drama of Æschylus, clearly foresaw all that was to befall him in consequence of his benevolent effort for the human race. Christ distinctly said that He was bringing, not peace on earth, but a sword; and He told His disciples that the time would come when whoever killed them would think he was doing God service. He repeatedly, early and late, warned men that whoever followed Him must follow Him carrying a cross. The cross here spoken of was not the pardon offered through His death, because Christ's death on the cross was yet future. It was not Christ's cross His follower was to bear, but his own. The cross was the punishment of slaves who rebelled against their masters. It was the byword of ignominious death, as rope, or halter, is with us. A man who set himself in hostility to the political, social, or ecclesiastical institutions of a country, would now be described as acting with a halter round his neck. This was precisely the idea that Christ conveyed to those who wished to become His disciples. He knew that He carried His life in His hand. If we refer to only one of his maxims of government, we shall see how reasonable were His calculations. He taught that the ruler should be servant of his people; that instead of thriving on their misery, he should suffer to make them prosperous. He Himself, He said, was the true shepherd, or ruler, because He would die for His people; and any man who assumed to rule, without copying this example, was a thief and a robber. He who, in any country the government of which is corrupt, teaches this doctrine—and to teach it is the essential part of the Christian preacher's duty—is carrying a cross, or whatever is the equivalent of a cross in the usages of his day. The sight of suffering caused by his example should not be represented as causing sorrow or disappointment to Prometheus. There cannot be a greater error than to impute such feelings to Christ. Nor need we entertain unmixed sentiments of horror at the inhuman wrongs that have been done in the name of religion. The privations endured by the teachers of truth, and asserters of man's rights, are the measure, it should be remembered, not only of human malice, but of human constancy and fortitude. Whenever an advocate and proclaimer of truth died at the stake, or on the scaffold, there was not only a cruel executioner, but a willing victim. Dreary and miserable as earth has been, it would have been far worse without its martyr. Persecution has only demonstrated that there are men who can dare unjust earthly omnipotence, and die.

And as to the superiority of defeated and afflicted goodness over goodness triumphant and prosperous in stirring those energies of the soul that lead mankind on to higher thoughts and acts, we may see it proved and exemplified in the high place which the "Prometheus Bound" possesses in the minds of men. We may also see it in the world's recoil from the religion of selfish prosperity. Popular Christianity hangs over an abyss of mere profession. This is only what might have been expected. Christ saw that corrupt laws and institutions usurped God's place and blotted out His justice. His primary object, therefore, was not to set men thinking about their souls in a future heaven, but to rouse every faculty of reason and righteousness to activity in establishing a heaven on earth. His followers, however, have almost universally preferred the shadow of His cross to the burthen of their own, and religion has lost its reality because it has lost its heroism. Shelley treated Christ only as the Christian world treated Him, and forgot that He was one who bruised His feet in making rough ways smooth, and was crowned with thorns for defining the true import of a crown, and was crucified because He exalted the empire of truth above the empire of force.

The final and most poignant torture is the description of mankind haunted by the spectres of a dead faith and mastered by the illusions of a corrupt society:

> In each human heart terror survives
> The ruin it has gorged: the loftiest fear
> All that they would disdain to think were true:
> Hypocrisy and custom make their minds
> The fanes of many a worship, now outworn.
> They dare not devise good for man's estate,
> And yet they know not that they do not dare.

The good want power, but to weep barren tears;
The powerful goodness want: worse need for them.
The wise want love; and those who love want wisdom;
And all best things are thus confused to ill.
Many are strong and rich, and would be just,
But live among their suffering fellow-men
As if none felt: they know not what they do.

To fulfil Shelley's standard of the noblest virtue he describes Prometheus as cleansed from all hatred by his sufferings:

I speak in grief,
Not exultation, for I hate no more,
As then ere misery made me wise.

. . . . . .

I am changed so that aught evil wish
Is dead within.

The earth is represented as saying to him:

Thou art more than god
Being wise and kind.

Even Jupiter when overcome exclaims:

Oh, that thou wouldst make mine enemy my judge,
Even where he hangs, seared by my long revenge,
On Caucasus! he would not doom me thus.
Gentle, and just, and dreadless, is he not
The monarch of the world?

The character of passionless goodness thus portrayed would be as incapable of affecting us as a star is of affording warmth, were it not that the poet is himself inspired by the vengeance which he denies to his hero, and inconsistently ascribes to him the exercise of hatred, even while he represents him formally as avowing himself free from its presence. The powerful opening address is full of concentrated hate, and is written to evoke abhorrence and detestation from the reader. The very curse which Prometheus had once pronounced, and now wishes to have repeated that he may recall it, is in reality introduced to give an opportunity of hurling defiance against the gods. Though Prometheus withdraws it on behalf of Jupiter, Shelley puts additional humiliation on Jupiter by making his phantasm recite it.

The liberation of Prometheus is at last produced by the progress of time hastened by love. Throughout the poem a special hour is expected as fraught with freedom. In the opening address Prometheus speaks of

> The wingless, crawling Hours, one among whom
> Shall drag thee, cruel King.

Again he says to Mercury—

> I wait,
> Enduring thus, the retributive hour,
> Which since we spake is even nearer now.

Asia goes to the cave of Demogorgon, who reveals to her the flight of the Hours:

> These are the immortal Hours.
> One waits for thee.

Demogorgon enters the chariot of the fatal Hour, ascends to heaven, and hurls Jupiter from his throne, falling with him into darkness. This invincible assailant of Jupiter is simply the result of the flow of events, the fructification of time, the spirit of revolution. Shelley thus symbolizes his belief that the certain and unceasing current of time would sweep priestcraft from the earth, and leave the heavens untenanted. The nature of Demogorgon is discernible in the description of his realm :—

Hither the sound has borne us—to the realm
Of Demogorgon, and the mighty portal,
Like a volcano's meteor-breathing chasm,
Whence the oracular vapour is hurled up
Which lonely men drink wandering in their youth,
And call truth, virtue, love, genius, or joy,
That maddening wine of life, whose dregs they drain
To deep intoxication ; and uplift
The voice which is contagion to the world.

When Jupiter inquires what he is, he replies :

Eternity. Demand no direr name.

And when Asia asks him who is the master of Jupiter, he answers—

If the abysm
Could vomit forth its secrets. But a voice
Is wanting, the deep truth is imageless ;
For what would it avail to bid thee gaze
On the revolving world ? What to bid speak

> Fate, Time, Occasion, Chance and Change? To these
> All things are subject but eternal Love.

Demogorgon, the bugbear of the Pantheon, the terrible god in the mystery of whose shadow the cheeks of all the other gods blanched, the inexorable law of development that will cleanse man's soul from all superstition, is impersonated by Shelley in order to cast Jupiter from his throne. As a person his work is then done, and he, too, passes into eternal darkness. But Shelley, with entire unconcern about dramatic proprieties, introduces him again in the fourth act to utter some further last words.

Mrs. Shelley, in her note on this drama, says that her husband followed certain classical authorities in figuring Saturn as the good principle, Jupiter the usurping evil one, and Prometheus as the regenerator. Shelley and Æschylus both agree in describing Saturn's reign as an early stage of knowledge and freedom. When a revolution impended that was to enlighten mankind, and improve their condition, Jupiter deceived Prometheus, the pure reformer, and seized the occasion to put himself on the throne. The first use he made of his power was to make the lot of man worse than before, if not to doom it to utter extinction. When Prometheus resisted, he impaled him.

Jupiter is the Cromwell, or Napoleon, of the skies. On the fall of Jupiter, Hercules liberates Prometheus, might takes the side of right, and the reign of happiness commences.

Shelley is intentionally oracular when he speaks of immortality. His theory is, that man is mortal, and the race immortal. Prometheus represents the race, and cannot die. If we compare Shelley's philosophy, which willingly resigns the individual body and soul to mingle with universal nature, with the modern sentiment, neither pantheistic nor Christian, which feebly shrinks from death, we discern a healthiness in its tone that the other lacks.

Flow down, cold rivulet, to the sea,
Thy tribute wave deliver;
No more on thee my steps shall be,
For ever, and for ever.

A thousand suns will stream on thee,
A thousand moons may quiver;
But not by thee my steps shall be,
For ever, and for ever.

. . . . . .

There's somewhat flows to us in life,
But more is taken quite away;
Pray, Alice, pray, my darling wife,
That we may die the self-same day.

Thus is morbid egoism—the soul's consciousness surviving the belief in its immortality.

Shelley's drama is crowded with irregularities, inconsistencies, and gross violations of almost every dramatic canon; but so infinitely rich and varied is the beauty of his poetry that we are unaware of any such imperfection. Who could turn away from the brightest flowers on which the sun ever shone, to ascertain whether the soil that bears them is cultivated according to the orthodox fashion? We lose our way at every step we take; but who laments at having lost his way, or wishes to recover it, or cares to learn whether there ever was a way to lose, when the byways in which he wanders are strewn with gems, and the air is resonant with the sweetest of music? The terrific monotone of the cataract thunders on the ear; and, when the startled sense erects itself to listen, it is wooed back to languor by the ripple of the rivulet and the song of the nightingale. The eye is perpetually changing its focus, as majestic distant forms and minute aspects of loveliness alternately and simultaneously claim the attention. The trumpet of the battle and the strain of the siren intermingle; the hard ascent and the luxurious grotto blend into each other. We travel through a primeval forest of giant trees, and our path is hindered by a wild underwood of blossoming shrubs and festoons of clustering vines. We are launched on a mountain lake, and our oars are entangled at every stroke by the stems of the water lilies. But we are not aware of any unfitness or incongruity. The strong wine is drugged with soporifics. Not only the scenic incoherencies, but the alleged immoralities and profanities of Shelley are lost sight of in the crowding wealth of his imagination. In other poetry, the snake is hidden in the verdure; in Shelley's poetry he is stifled.

In direct contrast to this is the tragedy of Æschylus. In it one figure of sorrow unrelieved, of majesty undiluted, fixes the eye and never allows it to wander. One thought holds the soul, and never relaxes its grasp. It is the triumph of stern simplicity. If viewed as a work of art, it is perfect beyond comparison; and if we seek to learn why it is so, we find it to be because it is simply true to nature. Its isolation and its fragmentariness have a mysterious lesson for us that we cannot fully explain to ourselves. If one looks on a map thickly covered over with names of towns and rivers, the mind passes over the surface on a level with its subject, and is stirred by no emotion. If a skeleton map with, it may be, one solitary spot marked on it as associated with the life and work of man, be contemplated, the mind is wrought to a different mood; we feel some secret of the soul is symbolized in the bareness of the promontories and the immensity of the ocean. If a plain covered with thick trees presenting a sea of foliage be regarded, the beauty of earth is seen, and our hearts drink in the joy. But if we look on a wide and wild and level moorland, with one solitary tree in its expanse, we are lifted, we know not how, to a higher sphere. What the skeleton map is to the crowded chart, and the solitary tree to the dense forest, the "Prometheus Bound" of Æschylus is to the "Prometheus Unbound" of Shelley.

HAMLET.

To make no allusion to the copious literature that exists on the play of "Hamlet" would be either to leave one's self without excuse for going beyond verbal criticism, or to assume the first discovery of the problem which has, in fact, engaged a host of writers. It is well known that the difficulty which has attracted so many commentators is owing to a supposed indistinctness in the character of the chief person, and to the inference that Shakspere meant to illustrate some principles or convey some lesson. If any such indefiniteness were observed in one of the historic plays, its cause would reasonably be sought in the necessary, fancy-filled interval that lies between the prose narrative and the poetic conception. But "Hamlet" is virtually an historical play. Traditions or fabulous legends must exercise as large a modification on dramatic compositions founded on them as established facts of history. This is mattter of observation as well as of probability. Let us sketch the history of Saxo Grammaticus, which suggested directly or indirectly the character of Hamlet to the mind of Shakspere.

In the reign of Roderick, two brothers, Horvendile and Fengon, were joint rulers of a province. The King of Norway challenged Horvendile to combat, and was slain by him. The conditions of the fight were that all the riches in the ship of the vanquished should pass to the conqueror. Roderick gave his daughter, Geroth, in marriage to Horvendile. Hamblet was their son. Fengon murdered Horvendile, and had sufficient address to gain condonement from the people and nobles, and even their consent to his marriage with his brother's widow. Hamblet, left friendless, counterfeited madness in order to elude his uncle and prepare revenge. He ran through the streets like one distracted, and spoke words of phrensy. Yet he sometimes acted and spoke in a manner that indicated a serious undercurrent of intention. Once he was observed sharpening sticks, and, when questioned, said that they were meant to avenge his father's death. The suspicion of the king and his courtiers being aroused, a beautiful woman, greatly beloved by the prince, was employed to entrap him into an avowal of his sanity and of the designs which he harboured. This attempt deeply moved him; but one friend whom he had gave warning, and the lady proved faithful. One of the courtiers, still full of misgivings, proposed to the king that Hamblet should have an interview with his mother, and offered to hide himself behind the hangings and hear the confidential communications the prince might make. The king assented. Hamblet, when summoned to his mother's chamber, suspected treachery, and imitating with his arms the flapping of a cock's wings, felt something move under the arras, and calling out, "A rat! a rat!" drew his sword, thrust it through, and stabbing the courtier, dragged him out and killed him. He then in a long speech denounced the unbridled passion of his mother in marrying her husband's murderer and ended by acknowledging that his madness was assumed, and that he meant to kill the king. The queen, moved by his reproaches, embraced him with affection, and made excuses for her conduct. When the king made inquiries concerning the slain courtier, Hamblet made answer that "the hogs meeting him had filled their bellies with him." Fengon resolved to put Hamblet out of his way; but not wishing to offend Geroth and the people, sent him to the King of England with two companions, who bore secret orders that he was to be put to death. Hamblet took his departure, having first requested his mother to hang the wall with tapestry, and to celebrate his funeral after a year had elapsed. During the voyage, while his companions slept, he substituted their names for his in their instructions. When he reached England, the king gave him his daughter in marriage, and hanged the two messengers. Hamblet feigned displeasure, and the king to appease him gave him a large sum of money, which he melted and hid in two staves. He returned to Denmark, and when asked about his companions showed the two staves, and said that those were they. The preparations for his funeral feast were applied with added zest to the celebration of his return; and, when the whole court were sunk in intoxication, he pulled down the tapestry on them, nailed it to the ground with the pointed sticks, and then set fire to the palace, thus destroying all his enemies save the king, whom he afterwards slew in his chamber after having *exchanged his own sword*, which his enemies fixed in the scabbard, for his. Hamblet then became King of Denmark, and was finally betrayed by his wife to another uncle, who slew him and married the traitress.

This account is compounded from the Roman

story of the first Brutus and popular tales of fools or half-witted persons who overcame powerful enemies by almost infantine devices. Such stories solaced the simple minds of oppressed peasants during centuries, and at last found a fixed and congenial receptacle in the nursery. Saxo Grammaticus worked the scattered fragments into form and dignified it with the name of history. The lower and unseen outline of this infertile rock, the exuberant genius of Shakspere has partly clothed with mould of his own invention, and altogether covered with the richest flowers and fruit of imagination. Those who are not satisfied with fruit and flowers, unless they are made to grow logically from a suitable soil, think there must be a hidden meaning in the incongruity. The same objection might be made in a less degree to every drama that Shakspere wrote.

Why, it has been asked, did Hamlet feign madness, and what purpose did it serve? Let us briefly compare the play with the history. Claudius killed his brother secretly; there is, therefore, no reason for Hamlet to fear that his uncle would suspect him of plotting vengeance, as the Hamblet of the history does, whose father had been killed openly. Accordingly, he consents not to go to Wittenberg, at his mother's request. The history and play differ in that the hero of the former feigns madness from the time of his father's murder, while the hero of the play feigns only after his father's ghost appears to him. The appearance of the ghost puts the Hamlet of the play in the same situation as the Hamblet of the history, and leaves him to be guided by the same motives and policy. The ghost makes the murder known to him, and binds him to secrecy by refusing to make the revelation save to him alone, and by sanctioning the oath of silence, which he imposes on Horatio and Marcellus. Hamlet, therefore, cannot openly kill Claudius, because the act would seem wanton and unprovoked. The only way left to him is through concealment and cunning. He guards himself against the newly-discovered danger and watches for revenge under the shelter of counterfeited insanity. The legendary Hamblet fears open violence from the known perpetrator of a murder, and pretends to be mad. Shakspere's Hamlet, grieving at his mother's hasty marriage, but free from apprehension of personal danger, as is evident from his consenting not to go to Wittenberg (i. ii. 120), suddenly learns that the king is the murderer of his father. This assimilated his circumstances to those of his prototype, and he instantly adopts the same disguise. He conceals the ghost's revelations from Horatio and Marcellus, because if it came to his uncle's ears it would be his interest to murder him likewise. Moreover, as the fact of his father's ghost having appeared to him, if known to Claudius, would at once suggest to his guilty conscience the object of the visitation, he solemnly pledges his companions not even by hint or innuendo to furnish any explanation of the "antic disposition" which he tells them he is about to put on. He pretends madness because he knows himself to be in the power of a criminal whom it is his duty to punish, but against whom he cannot proceed openly or publicly in consequence of the channel through which his information has come.

Various hypotheses have been invented to explain why Hamlet does not immediately kill Claudius. Goethe is of opinion that Shakspere's intention was to exhibit a pure but feeble soul staggering under the burthen of a task which it is unable to accomplish. Gervinus believes that he intended to exemplify the demoralizing influence and fatal results of philosophy, speculation, and conscientiousness as compared with immediate and resolute action. A number of medical writers maintain that Hamlet's irresolution is to be accounted for only on the theory that he was mad, not in pretence, but in reality. If these and other writers confined themselves simply to the facts they would see that Hamlet did not at once kill Claudius, or rather that Shakspere did not make Hamlet at once kill Claudius, because the poet's object was not to relate a single deed, but to compose five acts, and that with this view he has brought his plot into harmony with the original history, in which the hero does not immediately kill his enemy, but pretends madness, employs craft, and awaits his opportunity. Craft is the conventional weapon which tradition ascribes to assumed madness. Shakspere's Hamlet faithfully follows his prototype in the use of it. When Ophelia, after being forbidden to receive his overtures, is employed to betray him and worm out his secret, he retorts on his enemies and makes her the instrument of putting them on a false scent. The address with which he baffles Rosencrantz and Guildenstern, when they sound him concerning the ambitious views he is suspected of entertaining, and with which he turns Polonius into ridicule, is so successful a part of the representation that we cease to see in it an essential element in Hamlet's *rôle*, just as the grotesqueness in the gargoyles of an old church blinds us to their being not accessories or ornaments, but integral portions of the material edifice and speaking symbols of the ecclesiastical mind of the day. When he grows impatient as time advances and nothing is accomplished, it is his invention he appeals to—"About, my brain!" (ii. ii. 598, comp. v. ii. 30), and he hits on the device of the play. He kills Polonius, supposing he was the king, by craft, clearly showing how he meant to execute his purpose, and his readiness to kill Claudius when the occasion offered. A few lines from this scene show in what a mist of suspicion he dwells. Polonius has just gone behind the arras in the queen's chamber, and Hamlet enters. The queen says:

> Hamlet, thou hast thy father much offended.

Nothing would be more apposite than those words to lead to his subject if he did not apprehend that he was surrounded by treachery. He only echoes the charge:

> Mother, you have my father much offended.

Immediately afterwards, when he has slain Polonius and he no longer fears an eavesdropper, when the queen says,

> O what a rash and bloody deed is this!

he unreservedly pours out the full tide of his wrath :

> A bloody deed ;—almost as bad, good mother,
> As kill a king and marry with his brother.

He almost revels in the anticipation of circumventing the companions of his voyage to England :

> There's letters sealed : and my two schoolfellows
> Whom I will trust as I will adders fanged—
> They bear the mandate, they must sweep my way
> And marshal me to knavery. Let it work ;
> For 'tis the sport to have the engineer
> Hoist with his own petard : and 'twill go hard,
> But I will delve one yard below their mines,
> And blow them at the moon : O 'tis most sweet,
> When in one line two crafts directly meet.

When he returns from his frustrated voyage he boasts to Horatio of the way in which he outwitted his perfidious companions as the very sort of triumph alone within his reach ; and so far is Horatio from disapproving, as Gervinus to suit his theory would interpret, that after Hamlet's death he claims the credit of the act for him, when the ambassadors would ascribe it to the king. So closely does Shakspere associate the habit of retaliative subtlety with his hero's character, that when Osric comes with the king's message, Hamlet competes with him, and surpasses the exaggeration of his euphuisms, although he does not suspect the deadly treachery that lurked under its florid redundance. At last Claudius and Laertes encompass him with wiles from which escape is impossible. He falls, but not until he has slain them both by the recoil of their own artifice.

If it be established that the method imposed on Hamlet required delay, all the morbid fancies accounting for that delay on other grounds are shown to be foreign and fallacious. If all the legends concerning pretended madness agree that the object was to gain time in which to overreach or undermine, and if our play is constructed on the obvious framework of this idea, then the other explanations of the procrastinated revenge are shadows, and the theories built on them are baseless. It cannot be argued, in reply, that Hamlet, in some of his soliloquies, condemns his own apathy and spurs himself to more rapid movement. A poet's hero must rail at himself for not being able to overcome any obstacle that comes in his way. The Roman historian may describe Brutus as waiting patiently for his opportunity, Saxo Grammaticus may relate the childish preparations of Amlethus, but the Hamlet of Shakspere must rage in self-accusation against the necessity that binds him to inaction. How would the poet feel as he threw himself into Hamlet's part? Would he not chafe and storm at the slow progress of events? Is it not natural and customary to depict a great spirit hemmed in by the circumscribing sands of circumstance as raving in self-torture against the barrier, and ascribing to its own want of determination the laggard policy that is the acknowledged condition of its task?

There is a more important object than a strictly critical one in scattering those dreams of German commentators. They have assigned an immoral sense to Shakspere, in order to force him into agreement with their purpose. Poetry is forced to go in the crooked way of politics. Gervinus makes Hamlet a parable. "Hamlet is Germany." To show that the doom of Hamlet impends over Germany, unless she corrects her tendency to dissolve action in thought, it is necessary that this fault should be ascribed to Hamlet. Then for the correction of this fault an ethical maxim must be found; and, as it is assumed that Shakspere designed to convey the moral which Gervinus needs for Germany, the principle of conduct that should have guided Hamlet, and that Germany would be justified in adopting, must be found in Shakspere also. In the first interview between Hamlet and Rosencrantz and Guildenstern the following dialogue occurs:—

> HAM. Denmark's a prison.
>
> . . . .
>
> ROS. We think not so, my lord.
>
> HAM. Why, then, 'tis none to you; for there is nothing either good or bad, but thinking makes it so; to me it is a prison.
>
> ROS. Why, then, your ambition makes it one; 'tis too narrow for your mind (ii. ii. 236).

This sentiment, which is so familiar to us in the expression that stone walls do not a prison make, is thus commented on by Gervinus, whose theory is that Hamlet was deterred by over scrupulosity and a diseased conscientiousness from murdering the king:—

> Thus, from natural impulse and habit, the mind of this man of deep reflection is unconsciously the overruling agent in everything; thought has become with him the measure of things. Shakspere invests him with a philosophical principle, which contains a most characteristic modification of the poet's own worldly wisdom. That virtue and vice, good and bad actions, acquire no real importance in themselves, but ever from circumstances, objects, and natural character; that it is not the *what* but the *how* that decides the value of an action, is a maxim of Shaksperian experience, which is too frequently and too forcibly repeated in word and example, for the poet not to have always well weighed every word which he wrote in this sense. This maxim is thus modified in Hamlet's

lips: "There is nothing either good or bad, but *thinking* makes it so."[o]

As the end for which the parable of Hamlet was preached to Germany is now accomplished, we may, in view of even worse wrestings of more sacred texts, pardon the temporary adaptation and be satisfied with rescuing our bard from the imputation of an immoral maxim.

Shakspere did not write to inculcate special morals, or to delineate abnormal and exceptional formations of character. This belongs to lesser playwrights. Anyone may shape a career of fable to exemplify a principle. Only the sovereign mind can hold the mirror up to nature, and let the reflection teach its lesson as the realities of existence teach it. Shakspere is the poet, not of the oddities and imperfections of human nature, but of human nature itself with all its unexplained inconsistencies. His mystery is not the plot of a tragedy, but the mystery of life. The instruction mankind stands in need of is not fiction shaped artificially to a certain end in which poetic justice is wreaked on villainy, or one-sided instances of unprosperous vice or unfortunate weakness selected from the mingled sum

[o] Shakspere Commentaries, by Dr. G. G. Gervinus, 1873, vol. ii., page 136.

of things, but rather representative sections of human history just as it is, lifted before the public gaze and shone upon by the circumambient light of genius, so that every act and thought and circumstance stands revealed, and every beholder can draw his own moral and value it the more because it is his own. The ability to do this miracle is the rarest gift vouchsafed to men; and if in its largest measure it has been worked through the instrumentality of our English tongue, let us not prove ourselves unworthy of the distinction by classing our great poet, who teaches virtue by the display of universal nature, with inferior artists, who display only so much of nature as their limited conception of virtue will illustrate.

The medical critics are unanimous in pronouncing Hamlet really mad. This is merely a professional illusion. The mind dwelling on certain symptoms, projects them wherever it turns, just as the eye that has been fixed on a coloured outline will see it in the lucid blue of heaven. A legal friend said to me a few days since with energetic seriousness that if the affair of the rat behind the arras had been brought before a judge and jury the tragedy would probably be brought to a sudden and ignominious close. Dr. Conolly is enamoured of a French version in which, in the scene between Hamlet and his mother, the words of the ghost are omitted, and thus poor Hamlet seems raving mad, not only to his mother, but to the audience.

If indications of the design of Shakspere were decisive on this point there would be little room for doubt. If Laertes or Polonius had any suspicion that Hamlet was afflicted with insanity they would certainly make some allusion to it in the warnings they utter to Ophelia. It cannot be said they were unaware of it, or that it did not occur to them, because the question is: Would Shakspere, if he intended Hamlet to appear mad, keep the secret to himself, and never let it leak out in the speeches of any of the persons of the drama? Would he specify the time, the occasion, and the avowed intention of the pretence? Would he describe the ghost as acting in unison with and echoing to real madness? Would the king and queen speak of the suddenness of the change? Would Polonius enumerate all the symptoms as of recent occurrence? Those proofs, however, which might be added to from every speech in the play, are not really of avail, because the design of Shakspere does not decide the question. The common opinion is that Shakspere meant to describe a man pretending madness. The medical critics say that Shakspere described a man really mad. If we set aside the plain statement of Hamlet that he was about to put an antic disposition on, how can we possibly distinguish the assumption of madness from the reality? There is no way of representing a pretended madman but by making him like a real one. However successfully and accurately the writer finishes his portrait, we must still understand him as accomplishing that which he told us he meant to accomplish. The only way in which the medical writers can prove their case is by showing that Shakspere was mad, and this is in fact the legitimate and inevitable termination of their proofs, if they can prove anything. If Shakspere, after informing us that he was about to depict a pretended madman, drew a man really mad, there is only one way of accounting for the miscarriage.

No two things can be more distinct than the purposeless incoherency of Ophelia and the studied extravagances of Hamlet, under every sentence of which a pointed meaning is sheathed. Usage, not reason, is the test by which sanity is distinguished from insanity. Reason restrained, modified, and reduced to an average uniformity, regulates the sane man of public opinion. The man of pure reason, who should cast off the yoke of custom, would seem mad without being so; while the man of imperfect or disordered reason, who conformed to outward custom, would be mad without seeming so. Hamlet's madness was of the former kind. He describes the exact process by which he arrives at it immediately after the interview with the ghost:

> I'll wipe away all trivial fond records,
> All saws of books, all forms, all pressures past.

When the pressure of habit is removed, the established proportion of movement to motive, of action to passion, is lost. A man so circumstanced is in danger of being taken off his guard and hurried to excess if some strong and sudden emotion seizes him. Hamlet forgets himself for a moment at Ophelia's grave. He avows his love, and rivals the demonstrative sorrow of Laertes. Shakspere is careful to make him explain afterwards to Horatio that he lost the management of his simulated phrenzy for a moment, and let his natural passion carry him too far:

> But I am very sorry, good Horatio,
> That to Laertes I forgot myself,
>
> . . . .
>
> But, sure, the bravery of his grief did put me
> Into a towering passion.

Shakspere, in fact, was borne away by his vivid

impression of the scene, and, confident of the truth of its delineation, allowed it to remain, but reminds us that it was owing to a burst of natural passion unchecked by consideration of regard for appearance.

Hamlet's treatment of Ophelia is strangely misunderstood by the critics. His love for her was the main solace of his life after his father's death. When Polonius forbade her reception of his addresses he is keenly wounded, and makes a despairing effort to move her sympathy; and when she, having never really loved him, her strongest attachment being family affection, imputes his conduct to insanity, and joins her father in contriving snares for him, he pursues them with covert remonstrances and reproaches.

> POL. Do you know me, my lord?
> HAM. Excellent well; you are a fishmonger.
> POL. Not I, my lord.
> HAM. Then I would you were so honest a man.

Hamlet's apparently wild words are carefully laid to promote an occasion of uttering this retort on the man who was at that instant plotting against him. He continues:

> To be honest, as this world goes, is to be one man picked out of ten thousand.
> POL. That's very true, my lord.

HAM. For if the sun breed maggots in a dead dog, being a god kissing carrion,——Have you a daughter ?

POL. I have, my lord.

HAM. Let her not walk i' the sun : conception is a blessing ; but as your daughter may conceive,—friend, look to't.

In this way he ridicules the old courtier's extreme caution about his daughter's virtue at the very time when he was practising and teaching her to practise the most cruel treachery.

Again, when Polonius contrives the meeting between Ophelia and Hamlet, of which the king and himself are hidden witnesses, Hamlet, evidently aware of the plot, asks: "Are you honest ?" adding, "I did love you once." When she tamely replies, "Indeed, my lord, you made me believe so," he says, "I loved you not;" meaning that he did not love her in the character in which she now shows herself. Then he makes a last appeal to her sense of truthfulness: "Where's your father ?" and when she falsely answers, "At home, my lord," he pointedly says, "Let the door be shut on him that he may play the fool nowhere but in's own house!" He then breaks into general reproach, and seems to imply that the fashions of the day were frittering away the strength of true womanhood, and rendering the continuance of the race a questionable good. Thenceforward he makes no attempt to move her pity or her love. His conversation with her at the play is merely a specimen of the small talk of the time. The same remark applies to Ophelia's songs. There is nothing special to the relation between them in either.

It has been said that Hamlet was in advance of his rude era. This only means that Shakspere was a different person from Saxo Grammaticus. There are two Hamlets in the play, the Hamlet who acts and the Hamlet who thinks and speaks. Shakspere has walked on the northern wild, and the flowers of the south have sprung up in his footsteps. A shadowy outline of the subtlety with which oppressed innocence defended itself in primitive days is filled in with all the resources of a supreme intellect. If this were done designedly it would be consummate art. For the simplicity of Hamlet, in his grief, in his love, in his friendship, in his artifice, in his revenge, is brought home with hundred-fold, but ever undetected power to that inmost and deepest tenderness of every human soul, the remembrance and the remains of its childhood. In order to reconcile those two characters, the commentators have imagined one character misshapen and disordered.

But the same incongruity appears, as it could not but appear, in all the other persons of the play. The sage and beautiful counsel of Laertes to his sister rises far above the level of his character. The inimitable maxims of Polonius, which some critics, in their blind pursuit of consistency, have striven to depreciate, contrast with his subsequent follies. The spy Rosencrantz makes a majestic speech in defence of majesty (iii. iii.). It is impossible not to feel a pang of regret that a man who was so familiar with the sublimities of nature and the philosophy of political history, and could clothe his thoughts in such flowing verse as the gentleman or attendant (iv. v.) who brings news of the approach of Laertes attended by the rabble, should have filled so humble a position at the Danish court. Here is an instance of keen observation profoundly reflective, and of balanced conservatism haughtily contemptuous of popular encroachment, stepping with graceful dignity on the stage for a moment, and thenceforward immersed in obscurity. Was an ancestor of the poet a prisoner at the court of Claudius? Similarly, the first attendant in the same scene (not Horatio, as some copies read), who brings intelligence of Ophelia's derangement, shows a fineness of perception in the connection

9

between thought and language that proves him to have been a metaphysician and a grammarian, and a power of accurate survey of mental aberration that would do honour to a modern commissioner in lunacy. Is it not perverse ingenuity to seek for solutions of improbability and explanations of disproportion between form and substance in the work of a man who could not help turning whatever he touched into gold?

The soliloquies, it may be observed, are not properly integral parts of the tragedy. They are addresses to the audience explanatory and suggestive. They fill almost exactly the part of the ancient chorus. Ophelia (iii. i.) utters a soliloquy though she is aware that the king and her father are listening. The Dumb Show which should have affrighted the king, yet passes unnoticed by him, comes under this head. It was intended for the audience only.

The moral of "Hamlet" is artistic rather than ethical. The duty Shakspere set before himself was to write an effective play, a play that would glow in acting and entrance in hearing, a play that would stir with power the strongest passions of actor and audience. He has succeeded beyond measure. If we behold his creation from the front, suitably to its purpose, and judge by the potency of its skill upon us, we do not venture to criticise. But if we go behind the scenes and minutely examine the various parts, we only perplex ourselves with details, whose mutual relation and combined effect the creative mind of Shakspere alone could know. Every incongruity is explained by the general aim. Deep impressions are made not by continuity, symmetry, equipoise, but by flash and fragment and unexpectedness. We do not love smooth completeness. We love broken nature, rugged mountains, chequered sunlight. We have no fondness for tranquil demi gods and serenely secure virtue. Our hearts lean to imperfect men struggling to do right, and dying in the struggle. We are not held captive by Johnson's "Irene," or Addison's "Cato," or Milton's "Comus." We are held captive by "Hamlet." Here Shakspere has rung changes on every mood of the soul, solemn monotone, mirthful peal and jangling of sweet bells out of tune. If he has dealt sometimes with the ephemeral, it was that too great a strain might not be put upon us by thoughts beyond the reach of our souls. If he has played on the surface, it was that we might get relief from the long breathlessness of suspense. Each scene is a perfect study for the student who would understand or would describe human nature. The assemblage of scenes is kept in its place in the mind of the reader like a galaxy in the heavens. The personages, the interests, the events are brought near each other from the remotest spheres, and when we seek for the influences that group them they seem so subtle that we are not sure whether they were designed. If we are uncertain when we say that the whole play is bound and held together by delicate nerves of feeling, by abiding memories that constitute its identity, our doubt is allayed by remembering that nature, and every true imitator of nature, acts without our consciousness. The play is full of unseen unities.

The deterioration that takes place in the language and demeanour of Polonius, after the first act, is occasioned mainly by his accommodating himself to the supposed infirmity of Hamlet. He speaks sillily to him, just as we speak in broken English to a foreigner who does not know our language. The first scene in the second act, which is omitted on the stage, and is declared by the critics to have no share in furthering the plot, is a modification of the character of Polonius from the first exhibition of it, preparing the spectator for what is to come.

The device of Hamlet to assume madness, in

fact, disorders the whole course of events, and lands them on a declining plane that ends in the final catastrophe. The ghost is first to follow the wild motion. Polonius is shaken from his wisdom, the king from his calm, the queen from her apathy, Ophelia from her tranquil home life, Laertes from his youthful pleasures, and under its fatal influence all at last perish. If it be asked, Why does Hamlet die with the others? the answer is, that such must be the fate of the hero of a tragedy.

Perhaps the most constantly affecting circumstance in the whole poem, though, like the numberless other magic touches on our heartstrings with which it abounds, it eludes our notice, is the manner in which Hamlet, after Ophelia's rejection of him, reposes on the friendship of Horatio. There is nothing in nature so provocative of ineffable sympathy as a man compelled to unbosom himself to a man. It is because of this that the few cases of male attachment which history presents occupy so disproportionately large a place in our attention. "Thy love to me was wonderful," says David of Jonathan, "passing the love of women."

Hamlet's opening "aside" remark, "a little more than kin and less than kind," is the keynote to his future development. It is the germ from which expands the life of suppressed thought, relieving itself only in solitude; of environing danger from which he can escape only by subterfuges, of betrayed affection seeking alleviation in bitter irony. It prepares us for the victim to whom the heavens seem dark, and whom not man nor woman can delight.

Horatio introduces himself by the characteristic words, "A piece of him," and at once an expectant attitude is struck. We see one who does not exhaust his heart in words, who reserves his larger self for silent help, on whom will devolve at last the office of making clear all that his friend left unexplained.

The king's first lines tell us the manner of man that he is, and reveal the canker of his nature:

> Though yet of Hamlet our dear brother's death
> The memory be green—
> Yet so far hath discretion fought with nature,
> That we with wisest sorrow think on him,
> Together with remembrance of *ourselves.*

In this balanced and unabashed pretension of "ourselves" we see the selfish voluptuary and murderer. There is a vast difference between the man who is conscious of the instincts of selfishness and the man who has no shame in asserting them on a trying and solemn occasion. We at once know Claudius, and the knowledge grows on us till, when conspiring with Laertes to do a dastardly murder, he again says in excuse :

> I loved your father, and we love *ourself*,

and we see his base love lead him to his death.

When Laertes and Ophelia first appear before us, Laertes is just about to sail for France. He bids his sister farewell, and asks that he may hear from her. "Do you doubt that?" is her confiding and confident reply. There are a few women whose love, devoid of passion, dwells in deep and silent pools of home associations, that grow fuller and deeper each day, and never alters from the unquestioning trust of childhood. Their affection never runs over. They can love but once, for they can have no second father. Ophelia was one of these.

In the first scene, on the platform before the castle, the "honest soldier," Francisco, when relieved by Bernardo, speaks: "For this relief, much thanks: 'tis bitter cold, and I am sick at heart;" and he departs, never to appear again. But the memory of his words does not leave us. Like an obscure unlocalized pain, like a mournful echo, like a secret foreboding, they are felt midst every sound and heard in every pause ; and as the play advances towards the end we unknowingly crave for their solution. Like some mysterious syllable terminating a line in an irregular poem, they hang on our ears, and we watch with growing impatience for something that will rhyme to them, until at last, as the chill shadow of his approaching doom settles on Hamlet, he says to Horatio in words of saddest unburdening, "Thou canst not tell how ill all's here about my heart;" and we feel that we have at length plucked out the heart of the mystery.

THE BOOK OF JOB.

The Book of Job in its original form most probably ended with the present chapter xxxi. There is also great reason to conclude that the passage commencing with the thirteenth verse of chapter xxvii., and ending with chapter xxviii., was spoken by Zophar in the original poem. It is not my purpose to lay any stress on these or other alterations, or to inquire by whom they were made, or whether their object was to conceal or to disguise the author's primary lesson. I consider the book rather as a national composition than as the production of an individual.

The prose introduction to the poem gives an instance of the practical government of the world, and furnishes an explanation of the confusions that arise from the clashing of its physical and moral elements. Job is a virtuous and a prosperous man. God points him out to Satan, who presents himself along with the angels at the court of heaven, as an example of perfect uprightness. Satan replies that his integrity is not virtue, but self-interest, and that it would cease if his good fortune ceased. God permits Satan to put this accusation to the test; and Satan, by the agency of irruptions of plundering bands of enemies, the Sabeans and Chaldeans, of lightning and of tempestuous winds, destroys the family and the property of Job. The ruined man stands the ordeal, and admits God's right to take as well as to give. When Satan next appears amongst the angels, God again brings Job under his notice as one who was not only upright, but who had maintained his uprightness when "destroyed without cause." Satan alters his point of attack, and says that bare life furnishes a sufficient bribe to render the existence of virtue doubtful. Job's resignation was assumed only to save his life. If his life were threatened he would forsake righteousness. God gives Satan all power over him short of death, and Satan afflicts him with loathsome sores from the crown of his head to the soles of his feet. His wife taunts him with the worthlessness of his integrity, and bids him renounce it and die. Job remains firm. He acknowledges the sovereignty of God and virtue. He had received good from God's hand, and was ready also to receive evil. Thus Job establishes the existence and the power of perfect, disinterested virtue.

There are several axioms involved in the narrative which it is necessary to glance at. God and virtue are one. God is the impersonation of perfect virtue, and perfect virtue is the character of God. Happiness is the natural accompaniment and expectation of virtue. If happiness invariably followed virtue it would be an obstacle to its growth and to its recognition. The end of creation is the development of perfect virtue. God's supreme power divides itself into two kinds—moral and physical. The government of the world as a whole is ascribed to God. The physical government of the world is occasionally, or constantly with limitations, remitted to Satan. The moral government of the world is shared with men. God's ultimate sovereignty is not absolute power, but perfect wisdom, to which power is secondary and subservient. Satan arises in the evolution of virtue, and is made part of God's wisdom. That virtue may be perfect, man's will must be free. God's power is secondary to His wisdom, because the end sought is attainable by wisdom and not by power.

The mingled and mysterious world in which we live is the fruit of these principles. We may say generally that the world is of God; but when we speak of particular events we should attribute them to their particular and subordinate causes. The poetic portion of the Book of Job is a controversy on those topics. Truth is so distasteful to hear and so dangerous to speak that the poet puts a virtuous man to the rack in order that the boldness of his utterances may be ascribed to the extremity of his tortures.

The dwelling-place of God claims a moment's notice. It is well that men should have a correct idea of heaven before they accept or reject it. Heaven is commonly described as a region where spiritual Sybarites repose on uncrumpled doctrines, and rise to an eternal ascription of servile praises to the Almighty. The glimpse that we get in the opening chapter of Job reveals a different scene. We see no throned monarch lapped in ecstasy amid prostrate worshippers, but a busy Ruler filled with cares for His endangered kingdom. No strains of celestial melody float through lofty palace domes, but groans and cries and protests from earth reverberate through the antechamber of the King. When the material chaos settled into order the spiritual chaos began, and still continues. God is making heaven, and His call to us on earth is a call for help.

It is still more important to bear in our memories that it is not the quantity of Job's virtue that is under debate, but the quality of it. Satan never denied that the man who serves God for earthly reward and material happiness can give him a whole life's devotion. Nor are we to suppose that when God referred to Job's perfect uprightness He meant that he had never in any degree or at any time overstepped the limits of right. What God asserted and what Satan gainsayed was that "Job served God for nought." The question is not concerning the completeness of obedience, but concerning the genuineness of virtue. If goodness were not practised for its own sake, but for its attendant blessings, it would be prudence, policy, selfishness. Virtue calculating results would be undecided vice. It is the disinterestedness of virtue, therefore, the final purpose of creation, the triumph of God's wisdom, that is affirmed by God and contradicted by Satan. It is important, I say, to note this, because the two questions become confounded in the course of the argument.

When Job's three friends, Eliphaz, Bildad, and Zophar, heard of his calamities they came to mourn with him. During seven days they sat in silent sorrow, and then Job spoke. Like a wounded creature spending its rage on the weapon that pierces it, he curses the poisoned arrow, life, that quivers in his soul. With the measured cadence of despair he multiplies imprecations, and varies them with every throb of his anguish. His words are the mental echo to the actions of one who rings his hands, and smites them together, and clasps them in each other, as the spasms of endurance, impatience, and adjuration run their bitter round. Why was he ever born? Why did he not die in the hour of his birth? Why should life be forced on those who long for death? Words like these are only articulated groans. The friends of Job treat them as instances of rebellion and proofs of previous guilt. Eliphaz, strangely anticipating a taunt of later date, argues the insincerity of his righteousness from the fact that the topics through which he had formerly administered comfort to others were now found unavailing in his own case. Job's sorrows, it is inferred, must have sprung from his sin.

> Remember, I pray, who ever perished, being innocent?
> Or where were the righteous cut off?—(iv. 7.)

He then, in a passage whose poetical beauty has always been mistaken for healthy religious feeling, gives the experience of a disturbed and clouded conscience :—

> Unto me a thing came secretly,
> And mine ear received a whisper thereof.
> In thoughts from visions of the night,
> When deep sleep falleth on men,
> Fear came upon me, and trembling,
> Which caused all my bones to shake.
> Then a spirit glided before my face,
> The hair of my flesh stood on end ;
> It stood—but its form I could not discern ;
> A figure was before mine eyes ;
> There was a hush, and I heard a voice,—
> " Shall mortal man be more just than God ?
> Shall man be more pure than his Maker ?
> Lo ! in His servants He putteth no trust,
> And His angels He chargeth with frailty ;
> How much more those who dwell in houses of clay,
> Whose foundation is the dust ;
> Who are crushed before the moth-worm !
> From morning to evening they are destroyed :
> They perish for ever unregarded.
> Doth not their very excellency pass away ?
> They die, even without wisdom."—(iv. 12-21.)

It must not be lost sight of that the speaker is the antagonist of virtue and the advocate of a condemned cause. In the struggle between his earthly and his heavenly affections he has filled his soul with a mist of darkness and conjured up a shadow of terror that stands to him for a Person. Religion was meant to give us clear views of right, and not gloomy and indistinct visions of God. " Shall mortal man be more just than God ?" Than what God ? God has revealed Himself to man in sunlight as Justice. So far as man's soul is built on this model, he is more just than the indiscernible shape that appals and disorders the imagination of the superstitious dreamer. We must not be imposed on by the craft that strives to strike us dumb with the nomenclature of heaven, nor by the fanaticism which brandishes the name of God as fools toss firebrands. The allegiance we owe on high is due, not to the sound of a name, but to the sanctity of a character.

The theory of man's utter baseness is subservient to the doctrine that happiness is the object of life and the constant attendant on virtue, or what the men who hold this doctrine regard as more than the equivalent of virtue, the confession of our depravity. "Confess yourself a sinner," Eliphaz says, " and God will restore all that you have lost."

Job had not hitherto served God for reward, and he will not now depart from the principle of his life. To do so would be to forsake God for Satan, for the contest concerning him was whether he was righteous for righteousness' sake, or for the increase of his substance. He again asks for death:—

> O that I might have my request,
> And that God would grant my desire;
> That God would resolve to crush me—
> Would stretch out His hand and cut me off!
> Then would I yet have the consolation,
> And could exult over this unsparing anguish,
> That I have not violated the Commandments of
> the Holy One.—(vi. 8-10.)

Then Bildad takes up the argument, and insists on the antecedent principle that God is just, and that, therefore, whatever He does must be admitted as just. Since He slew Job's children, they must have sinned, because He destroys none but sinners; and since Job was afflicted, he cannot be innocent, because the innocent are never afflicted.—(viii.)

To this Job answers that he knows that God is just, but that the manifestation and sphere of His justice are unknown. The current idea of divine justice was taken not from the moral instinct, nor from a true induction, nor from revelation, but from the foregone conclusion that prosperity is the mark of virtue, and adversity of vice, which was the very point at issue. This notion left the action of justice or the nature of virtue in uncertainty; for if it can be shown that a guilty man ever prospers, then guilt is indistinguishable from innocence, or else justice must be administered on some unknown principle. Job's argument enforces the latter alternative—

> This one thing I affirm,
> That the upright and wicked He alike destroyeth;
> When the scourge slays suddenly,
> He laughs at the trials of the innocent.—(ix. 22.)

Is power justice? Then this puts an end to all discussion and reasoning, which are pre-supposed and allowed by our primary conception of justice. The universe is alive with God's power; but He passes me by, and I see Him not. He will not deign to reason with me. He overwhelms me with the tempest of His fury. We listen for His voice, and we are stunned with the thunder. We look for light, and we are dazzled by the flash. With yearning, anxious souls we ask a question about virtue and suffering, and we are told that God made the heavens. What has this to do with our question? The power to make a thousand heavens could not give the right to lay one sorrow on an innocent spirit. If the power that created the stars can heal the mourner's grief, why is it all lavished on inanimate matter? And if it cannot, what is it to me that through immeasurable space suns stand self-balanced and planets revolve?

It were better to consign the mechanism of creation to independent law, and bring back God among men, than to describe Him as guiding planets, and give this as a reason why we are to groan unpitied. If injustice reigns on earth, how can the surging doubt of the soul be quelled by being informed that God made the Pleiades and the Chambers of the South? Will it ease my pang to learn that the hand that inflicts it made Arcturus and Orion? Power, so far as I have seen it, is associated with wrong. Show me God trusting in right and suffering from might, as I do, and He will reason with me. Such is Job's cry.

Men say it is well with the righteous and ill with the wicked. But this is an innate conviction, not an inference from observation. We are persuaded of it, and cling to it in darkness, despair, and death; but it lacks confirmation from visible experience. When we come to facts, how are we to discern the righteous man? Are we to argue back from appearances? This would be proving that the prosperous man is righteous, not that the righteous is prosperous. To make the proposition logically sound we should have the good man first indicated, and then behold prosperity following his path. God does not do this. We cry to Him in our agony, and ask what sin has brought our sorrow, and He heeds us not. There is no use, therefore, in appealing to foundations that are hid in the abysms. It is better to shelter our moral instinct from the world, to let it live in the one region where it can live, and there await a time of expansion, than to expose it prematurely to the chill of casuistry and the irony of facts.

The award of power cannot be a solution of moral anomalies. The thunder and the earthquake cannot drown the still small voice. If the good man suffers and complains, he is pronounced a sinner for complaining. But if he was good and suffered undeservedly, he was justified in complaining. The question is, was he good? Power cannot answer, has no right to answer.

This reference of moral difficulties to Divine power is echoed back to earth in ceaseless reverberations. After having said that God laughs at the temptations of the innocent, Job proceeds:—

> The earth is given unto the hand of the wicked:
> He covereth the faces of its judges;
> If it be not He, who, then, is it?—(ix. 24.)

All the tyrannies of earth are shadows of the asserted tyranny of heaven. Henceforth we cannot be shocked at any seeming profanity in the language of the poem, because we see that it is levelled against human injustice—against the godless vicegerent of God, whose bribed priests celebrated a despot god that human despotism might seem a godlike institution. If God's power be justice, if whatever God does is just because He is able to do it, and if human government be an ordinance of God, then human government is founded on might, and man's duty is to suffer wrong without complaint or inquiry. The theory of God's character affects not merely our religion; it affects every earthly institution. The problem of disinterested virtue is not a speculation of idle philosophy: it enters into all the relations of life, and is decided in every adjudication of human authority. If might be right, and the ruler's unjust decision must not be questioned, then all obedience for conscience' sake is abolished, and self-interest becomes the only motive that remains to regulate human conduct. We cannot wonder that men who had God set before them as the pattern of brutal kings and lawless conquerors should have endeavoured to blot Him from heaven.

Zophar appeals to God's secret knowledge as furnishing a reason for Job's afflictions. He concludes from the *unknown* that he is guilty. Let him repent and all will go well with him.

This means, let him not serve God for nought; let him cease his vain obedience to a righteous god who cannot save him, and transfer his allegiance to a god of power and rewards.—(xi.)

In his reply Job lays bare the root of the false argument of his friends. He had already pleaded as an argument against the pretensions of power, that a god of mere power could make him appear guilty whether he were so or not by overwhelming him with disasters that common opinion identified with guilt.

> I know that thou wilt not acquit me.
> I must be accounted wicked:
> Why, then, should I labour in vain?
> Should I wash myself in snow water,
> And cleanse my hands with rock,—
> Yet wouldst thou plunge me in the ditch,
> And mine own clothes would abhor me.—(ix. 28-31.)

If men would persist in making calamity the token of sin, and appealing to a god of power to justify their judgment, such a god could always confute the arguments of righteousness by arraying it in loss and misery. Righteousness in itself and for itself is an independent and incomparable good. This is God's original position illustrated by Job's life and now maintained by his arguments. Satan and Job's friends strive to represent the love of righteousness as the love of prosperity, and thereby seek to destroy the essence of right, making it consist only in its visible accident. But we may easily see how unjust this judgment by appearance is.

> Peaceful are the tents of robbers,
> And they that provoke God are secure;
> Into whose hands God bringeth abundance.—(xii. 6.)

The beasts of the field prey on each other, the fierce and cruel on the weak and harmless, and God suffers it. There may be, no doubt there is, a secret wisdom in this; but on the strength of the unknown explanation we must not infer that robbers are more righteous or more favoured by God than their victims, or that lambs are guiltier than tigers. It may yet be revealed to us why cruelty triumphed and innocence was overthrown; but this possibility is not to prevent us from pronouncing innocence to be innocence and justice to be justice. We know as an abstract principle that God is just, and we know with equal certainty that just men suffer: are we to wait for the unfolding of the mystery, or cut the knot now by confounding justice with injustice? There is a true sense in which all things and events are attributable to God—a sense consistent with the absolute wisdom of His character. But there is also a false ascription of authority by which men adulate the omnipotence of heaven. We are all familiar with the pious platitudes, the supine commonplaces, of popular religion. He breaketh down, and none can rebuild. He misleadeth counsellors, and maketh judges fools. He increaseth nations and destroyeth them. He blinds rulers and maketh them reel like drunkards. —(xii. 13.) The commercial shock that vibrates through the civilized world has a magnitude commensurate with God's majesty. But take it in detail: go into a single desolated home, look into one despairing heart, contemplate one ruined life, and will you say that is God's deed? The victory that decides an empire's destiny is ordained of heaven; but take one murdered victim of ambition, and will you dare to say that God was the murderer? The conquest was made in the might and the wisdom of the Lord; but behold a solitary, demoralized, unhumanized, imbruted slave, and say is that God's handiwork? The earthquake, the famine, the storm, the sack of the city, the wreck of the ship are from God; but the ruined home, the profaned altar, the shrieking maiden? The wars of tribes and nations, and the pestilence that walketh in darkness, rise to proportions worthy of Deity; but behold Job sitting in ashes childless and anguish-riven!

Do we not see that our ascriptions of honour to God are the echoes of our lies to our fellow-men? We flatter God as man is flattered. We call the wholesale murderer a hero, and we treat God so. We call the spoiler of a continent a statesman, and we treat God so. We rank Jehovah, the omnipotent, with Alaric the destroyer and Alexander the Great.

> Will ye speak wickedly on behalf of God,
> And argue deceitfully on His behalf?
> Will it be good when He searcheth you out,
> If ye flatter Him as man is flattered?
> Surely He will reprove you,
> If ye secretly be partial.
> Should not His majesty fill you with reverence,
> And His dread fall upon you?
> Your memorable sayings are dust;
> Your strongholds strongholds of clay.—(xiii. 7-12.)

This slavish indiscriminating homage proves how unworthy is our conception of Him to whom we offer it. There is an Order within this chaos, a Providence within this confusion, a God of living justice within this blind unsympathizing fate; to Him Job addresses himself:—

> So He may slay me, I may cease to hope,
> Yet to His face will I defend my ways;

He, too, shall be my deliverance,
For the hypocrite cannot come into His presence.
(xiii. 15, 16.)

He feels with an invincible conviction that there is a clue to this maze, though he cannot lay his hand upon it. He knows with the certitude of consciousness that there is a light in which all could be made clear. He is as sure as he exists that if he and his accusers stood now before God, he must be acquitted, and they condemned. The elucidation of the mystery is in the nature of things. It may yet burst forth into daylight, but he shall not be there to see it. He would be satisfied if in the future for a single instant he could be summoned from the blank of non-existence, to witness the vindication and the triumph of right.

There is hope of a tree,
If it be cut down, that it will sprout again,
And its tender branch not fail :
Though its root in the earth wax old,
And its stock in the soil die,
Yet will it bud at the odour of water,
And shoot forth boughs as when planted :
But man dies and wastes away ;
Man breathes his last, and where is he ?
Waters pass away from a lake,
And a stream is parched up and dries ;
So man lies down and rises not

Till the heavens be no more they shall not awake,
Nor be roused from their sleep.
Oh that Thou wouldst hide me in sheol,
Wouldst conceal me till Thine anger turn,
Wouldst appoint a time and remember me,
All the time of my warfare would I wait
Till my time to be relieved cometh,
Then Thou wouldst call and I would answer Thee.—
(xiv. 7-15.)

The contemplation of a total end of existence had a different effect on Job's mind from that which it has on ours. He had never been accustomed to indulge in any other view. He had never relaxed his mental vision with the prospect of an eternal redress. So the end of life was not a ground of sadness or disappointment, but a stimulus to redoubled remonstrance. When his earthly hope perishes, he cannot sit in contentment awaiting the resurrection. It is not the restoration of his personal happiness he thirsts for, but the justification of his trust in a righteous God. So he must forthwith lift his voice against wrong. We who have been familiarized with the hope of immortality have blinded our moral vision by constantly gazing upon it. All wrong and outrage is beheld with indifference, because there is an endless futurity of reparations. We have lost the distinctness and right value of present things by gazing into an incomprehensible distance. We have melted the pearl justice in the goblet of eternity. We have evaporated the rounded dew-drop of our morning conscience into the impalpable azure. We have wasted the beam of the candle of the Lord within us, that was given to guide our steps, by striving to mingle it with the radiancy of invisible suns. We suffer, and see our brother suffer, injustice, and are content, because it will be set right hereafter. But if we lose our sense of justice, nothing can ever be set right for us. And we have almost lost our sense of justice and our impatience with injustice; and in consequence, when modern science turns our dawn into darkness and destroys our hope of another life, we have no faith or hope left for earth or heaven. Our argosy has sailed on the vast ocean, and it is lost. It comes to us no more. We staked the justification of God on the reality of a future judgment, and in His anger He suffers it to vanish from our eyes. We despair of earth and heaven. The only God that remains for us is the God of injustice; the only principle that remains is the principle of selfishness. Our sympathies are with Satan and his three supporters, who scorn and calumniate the man who serves God for nought. Job's theology was a healthier one than ours. It would be better for us to lose our belief in immortality and retain our integrity and a grand implicit faith than to retain belief and lose our moral sense, for the moral sense *is* immortality. It is better to be immortal than to say "I believe in the resurrection of the dead."

In their next series of addresses Job's friends accuse him of irreverence, repeat that the heavens are not pure in God's sight, much less corrupt and abominable man (xv.), and dilate on the irreversible downfall of the wicked (xviii.–xx.) The question under debate is whether man is a slavish, degraded being, who can do no better thing than confess his abject worthlessness and accept the earthly happiness of which alone he is capable, or whether he is righteous and unrewarded. Confess your vileness, be happy, and so still the heart's longings, and solve the problem of life, said the orthodox party in Job's time. Job, on the contrary, asserted his righteousness, that is, the disinterestedness of his virtue, when he was shorn of every earthly joy, and so made existence appear an unfinished history, an uncompleted syllogism. When the doctrine of immortality was made known, the believer in temporal prosperity as the reward of religion could imagine no other world than a continuation of this, while the asserter of righteousness beheld the fulfilment of his vague desire and the solution of his difficulty. The mass of religious men in all ages, believing that the acknowledgment of man's entire corruption wins earthly favour from God, conceive, in consequence, a heaven from which every spiritual nature revolts. Orthodoxy has been made to consist altogether in belief apart from the quality of the things believed in, until disbelief in those things has become a negative proof of aspiration more satisfactory to the hopes of the human soul than the consent of all the churches. The counsels of heaven are forced into accommodation with earth such as Satan, by the aid of the Chaldeans, the Sabeans, and the brute forces of nature, has made it; and heavenly mansions are furnished for those who never entertained an unearthly or an unselfish thought. The picture drawn by the friends of Job is no dream. There is, beyond doubt, a safe prosperity and a substantial happiness on earth. It is for him who restrains the extravagance of his vices and his virtues, the former just below, the latter just above, the level of prudent management and public observation. This man has the world at his feet. He provokes no lightning, and the Sabeans know him as their brother. He confesses that he is a sinner, and Satan puts him to no trial. We need not suppose that the comforters of Job were exactly of this type, but unquestionably their arguments rested on such men, and tend to multiply them. And the affliction which they associated with what they called wickedness was, and ever will be, realized in men of Job's character. They do not seek rewards, and it is Satan's special office to take care that they do not get them, for, if they did, their example and their influence would weaken too much the discipline of life. Meanwhile the sight of their wrongs rouses and stimulates every generous spirit:—

> Mine eye is dim through vexation,
> And all my limbs are as a shadow.
> At this the upright are astonished,
> And the innocent rouses himself against the impious.
> But the righteous shall hold fast his way,
> And the pure of hands increase strength.—(xvii. 7-9.)

Eliphaz, in his third and last address (xxii.), nakedly avows the selfish doctrine of morals, which follows logically from the one-sided contemplation of God's omnipotence. The writer manifestly aims at exposing to detestation the fashionable religion of his day by confessing, in the words of one of its advocates, the mean profanity of its principles:—

> Can a man be profitable to God,
> As a wise man is profitable to himself?
> Is it a pleasure to the Almighty that thou art just?
> Or gain to Him that thou makest thy ways perfect?
> Through fear of thee will He plead with thee?
> —(xxii. 2-4.)

If we regard God's righteousness, we can be a profit and a pleasure to Him. For what is history but a continual cry for help from defeated virtue? But if we exclusively regard God's power, we cannot be profitable to Him. In the first case, we do what we can for God; in the second, we get what we can from Him. Here we have distinctly and briefly the two systems of morals, God's and Satan's. Eliphaz and his followers, looking only at God's power, say, naturally enough, What profit can your goodness be to God? They regard goodness, not as a contribution to some wise universal end, but simply in relation to the happiness of the individual. And as earthly happiness does not need goodness as an ingredient, they disavow it, confess themselves sinners, and trust in God's power. Having justified their prosperity by this process of reasoning, they argue backwards from the adversity of the truly just man in a totally different direction :—

Is not thy wickedness great ?
Are not thine iniquities innumerable ?
For of thy brother thou hast taken a pledge for nought,
And stripped off the clothing of the destitute ;
To the weary thou hast given no water to drink ;
And hast withholden bread from the hungry,
As if the land belonged to the man of power alone,
As if only the man of rank may dwell therein.
—(xxii. 5-8.)

If you confessed yourself to be a sinner, the argument runs—God would cause you to prosper ; but you do not prosper, therefore you *are* a sinner, abusing that very power which you disclaim and opposing the poor whose friend you profess to be. Such was the orthodox mode of reasoning in Job's time. Disinterested virtue is a delusion. It will expose you not only to misfortune, but to the charge of the wrong and high-handedness which you scorn and hate. There is no virtue or goodness but that which stipulates with the power of God for the wages of prosperity :—

If thou return to the Almighty, thou shalt be built up.
Thou shalt put away iniquity from thy tabernacle ;
Then shalt thou lay up gold as dust,
And the gold of Ophir as the stones of the brooks ;
And the Almighty shall be thy defence,
And thou shalt have plenty of silver.—(xxii. 23-25.)

You charge my doctrine, Job answers, with tyranny and oppression of the weak. Your doctrine of selfishness is the triumphant one: behold its fruits in the desolation and wretchedness that fill the land:

The wicked remove landmarks;
They drive off flocks and feed thereon.
The ass of the fatherless they drive away;
They take the widow's ox for a pledge;
They turn the needy from the way,
The poor of the land must hide themselves together.
So they go forth, like wild asses in the desert to their work,
Seeking diligently for food;
The desert their children's bread!
In the field they reap his corn,
And crop the oppressor's vineyard;
Naked they pass the night unclad,
And without a covering in the cold;
They are wet with mountain showers,
And for lack of shelter embrace the rock;
The wicked snatch the fatherless from the breast,
And take in pledge what is on the poor;
They cause the naked to go without clothing,
And hungry are they who bear the sheaves;
Within dark walls they cause them to press oil;
They tread winepresses, yet suffer thirst.
Here from the city men are groaning,
There the soul of the wounded crieth out;
Yet no judge regardeth the supplication.—(xxiv. 2-12.)

And what is the possession for which this price is

paid? Who and what are the few for whose exaltation the many are sacrificed? Does the God of power, whom alone they recognise, impart to them of His own attributes? Does He make them immortal?

> They are exalted for a while—and are not.
> They are cut off like topmost ears of corn;
> They die like all beside.—(xxiv. 24.)

Bildad, who closes the controversy on his side, can only restate his exhausted argument in exaggerated terms that expose its disjointedness and inconsequence:

> Dominion and terror are with him;
> He worketh absolutely in His high places.
> How, then, can man be just before God?
> The moon and stars are not pure in His sight:
> How much less frail man, a worm,
> And the son of man, a reptile.—(xxv. 2, 5, 6.)

So religious men reasoned then, and so they reason now. Let us attend to Job's answer.

You say God is mighty, and you ask me how can man be just before Him? Man can be just before the God of might, because the power of justice, which you ignore, is mightier, holier, than the power of might. When you speak of God's power you do not comprehend the meaning of your words. You confine your view to what is without you, and you lose sight of God's grandest work. "He worketh absolutely in His high places!" Yes, He stretches the north over empty space, He hangs the earth upon nothing, He binds the waters in His clouds, He hushes the sea, He garnishes the heavens—But what are these things? They are but the outskirts of His ways, the whisper of His voice. The thunder of His power, which you cannot understand, is the eternal law of justice echoed in the heart of man. One moral impulse is greater than the movements of all the sidereal heavens:—

Look then abroad through nature to the range
Of planets, suns, and adamantine spheres,
Wheeling unshaken through the void immense;
And speak, oh man! does this capacious scene,
With half that kindling majesty dilate
Thy strong conception, as when Brutus rose
Refulgent from the stroke of Cæsar's fate,
Amid the crowd of patriots; and, his arm
Aloft extending, like eternal Jove
When guilt brings down the thunder, called aloud
On Tully's name, and shook his crimson steel,
And bade the father of his country, hail!
For lo! the tyrant prostrate on the dust,
And Rome again is free!

Akenside's *Pleasures of Imagination*, Book I., 487.

Having distinguished the moral from the material majesty of God, Job once more asserts the rectitude of his principles, and his determined maintenance of them. It will be recollected that what he calls his righteousness is not perfect goodness, but goodness, so far as he had it, of an unselfish kind. So far as he served God he served Him without covenanting for reward. He proves this by holding his position unchanged even in the presence of God, who had neglected him and treated him unjustly. To abandon it would be to fall away from righteousness:

> As God liveth, who hath neglected my cause,
> Till I expire I will not relinquish my integrity;
> My righteousness I hold fast and will not let it go.
> —(xxvii. 2, 5, 6.)

The acknowledgment of sin which Satan and his friends wished to wring from Job was the confession that his virtue was hypocrisy. This he will never admit. His virtue was pure love of right and God. In the strength of that love, amid the wreck and ruin of his fortunes and the tortures of disease, he can stand in the presence of his Maker unabashed. This is the real power of God. Can the impious man, or he who serves for reward, do this? Can he stand before the Power in which he trusted? Did he delight himself in the Almighty? Was he not merely an expectant upon power? That power will not save him from death, nor his posterity from poverty and destruction. So little does omnipotence, apart from justice, effect for its votaries.

And why, Job continues, do you attempt to cow and crush men's hearts by introducing the works of creation into the argument? There is no analogy between the moon and stars and man's soul that you should compare them or argue from one to the other. Man digs in mines, but cannot find wisdom there. He cannot find it in earth or sea. Why cannot he find it? Because the wisdom by which God rules the inanimate world is a different wisdom from that by which He rules the rational soul of man. God portions out to His different creations their different wisdoms. He gave weight to the winds, and measured out the waters; made a course for the rain, and a path for the thunder-flash. And to man He said: "Lo! the fear of the Lord, that is wisdom."

Having thus refuted his adversaries, Job, in a lengthened discourse, repels their insinuations by showing how he had faithfully discharged all the duties that purity and charity demand from man. Thus the opponents of righteousness are conclusively overthrown.

But the victory has been too overwhelming, the strain has been too great, the flight of virtue has been at too lofty a height and too far away from the legitimate attractions of earth. As Job's friends erred in singling out God's power for the sole object of consideration, so Job was necessarily compelled in his answer to dwell too exclusively on His justice. In his scorn at their sordid trust, Job seemed to lose sight of the fact that a divine attribute was under discussion. Though God's justice is greater than His power, His power also must be vindicated. Virtue must not be left denuded of happiness. Vice cannot be left in possession even of earth. Men must not be tempted to mistake adversity for virtue by their constant companionship. The weak must not be discouraged; the strong and the hypocrite must not be emboldened.

In the subsequent part of the poem a new speaker appears, who censures Job's friends for not refuting him, but adds nothing to their arguments. Then God speaks, and Job humbles himself before Him, and has all that he lost restored twofold. This teaches us that however we may renounce the slavish doctrines of men we must reverence God in our hearts, and that an unspeakable blessing remains for those who love the right for its own sake. Still we must in no degree lose sight of the design of the poem, which is to establish the rights of man here and his hopes hereafter on the immovable foundation of the reality of virtue and a true conception of the divine character.

FABLES.

The fable, or that most ancient form of it in which the power of speech is ascribed to the lower orders of creation, is supposed by some writers to have naturally originated in that part of the world where the transmigration of souls was believed in. Others regard it as a dreamy reminiscence of the Golden Age, when man, beast and trees met and conversed with each other on terms of mutual understanding and amity. It is more reasonable to suppose that fables are simply a result of the effort which man has always been making to express his thoughts suitably and forcibly. Just as single words such as "mountain," "star," "lion," "oak," were used to express figuratively simple ideas of character, so those figurative words were grouped together to describe more complicated relations of conduct. The oldest known fable extant is that called Jotham's parable, in the ninth chapter of Judges. Anyone who reads the whole narrative will see how naturally the occasion prompted the utterance, and will also find grounds for inferring that fables indicate rather a different trait between man and the lower animals, than an identity as implied in the transmigration of souls—in reality require a wide difference between them, for they often are, in fact, parodies on the actions of man. Jotham's parable is as follows: "The trees went forth on a time to anoint a king over them; and they said unto the olive-tree, Reign thou over us. But the olive said unto them, Should I leave my fatness, wherewith by me they honour God and man, and go to be promoted over the trees? And the trees said to the fig-tree, Come thou, and reign over us. But the fig-tree said unto them, Should I forsake my sweetness and my good fruit, and go to be promoted over the trees? Then said the trees unto the vine, Come thou, and reign over us. And the vine said unto them, Should I leave my wine which cheereth God and man, and go to be promoted over the trees? Then said all the trees unto the bramble, Come thou and reign over us. And the bramble said unto the trees, If in truth ye anoint me king over you, then come and put your trust in my shadow; and if not, let fire come out of the bramble, and devour the cedars of Lebanon." Jotham's fable illustrates the general rule that where irrational or inanimate actors are introduced, the meaning is got, not by considering their natures, but by keeping in mind the characters of the persons whom they represent. Human motives are in an arbitrary and unjust way ascribed to beasts or trees, and then the names of the tree or beast, associated with ridicule or condemnation from such ascription, are reflected back on the human agent. Nobody would ever think of calling a bramble contemptible or tyrannical until it had been identified with a contemptible or tyrannical man. Its fruit is not so valuable as that of the other trees, but then its growth and attitude are correspondingly humble. As to the vine, I should like to have Sir Wilfrid Lawson's opinion about it. It is because low-minded men are frequently arrogant that the lowly bramble has arrogance ascribed to it. Similarly in the fable of the mountain in labour; the mountain is made ridiculous by describing it as doing metaphorically what only bombastic and self-important men do. We must not, therefore, insist too much on the supposed intrinsic characters of the actors in fables. Thinking of the private character of a tragedian would not help us to understand his delineation of Hamlet. So thinking about the personal character of a preacher might not assist us in comprehending his discourse. I know some people hold a different idea on this subject, but the world is full of prejudices and errors. But to come back to Jotham's parable, it reminds us of the proverbial saying, "That if you set a beggar on horseback he will ride in the wrong direction." This proverb, which is a fable put hypothetically, is very unjust towards beggars. If you were literally to put a beggar on horseback, the great probability is that he would fall off. The intended meaning is that if a person unaccustomed to the control of large sums of money were suddenly placed in a position where unlimited wealth lay at his disposal, he would be sure to run a career of extravagance. This may be quite true, but there is no reason why a beggar rather than a town councillor should be selected as the illustration of it. Jotham's parable had a political meaning. Communities seek for good men to have rule over them, because they know that good men in office will do their duty, and sacrifice their own comfort to the welfare of the community. On this very account sincere and honest men shrink naturally from taking office. No one is anxious to thrust himself into a position in which he is bound to forget himself and think only of others. But mean and selfish men are always anxious to rule, because they have a wrong estimate of the ruler's duty, and think only of themselves and wish to be tyrants. This was what Jotham intended to imply by calling Abimelech a bramble. That curious superstition that treats the maxims of the Bible as objects of blind adoration, and not of practical use, keeps this parable too much out of sight. We see from it that politics were just the same thousands of years ago that they are to-day. Whenever there is an election of any kind, this is what happens: A deputation waits on the olive-tree, and invites him to reign over them, and the olive says, Do you suppose I'm going to forsake the service of God and man, and betake myself to a place where neither God nor man is served or respected? Then the offer is made to the fig-tree, and the fig-tree answers, I won't give up my sweetness and good fruits, and mix myself up in affairs where sweetness and good fruits would be utterly thrown away. Then the vine is invited, and the vine says, No; thank you; I'm fond of respectable society, and I don't wan't to be seen among the democrats of the alliance. So at last they go to the bramble, and the bramble says, Yes, I'll be the Lord's anointed; and if anyone disobeys my orders, I'll provide coals enough to set these men on fire.

The fable of Menenius Agrippa, which we meet with in early Roman history, may be taken as a counterpart to that of Jotham. The Plebeians had risen in insurrection against the Patricians, and Menenius made them ashamed of themselves by telling them that they acted as foolishly as the members of the human body would act if they were to conspire against the stomach and refuse to supply it with food on the ground that it did nothing in return. Now it might have been argued in reply that the stomach sometimes does its work badly, and sometimes undertakes more work than it is able to perform; but it did not occur to the Plebeians to say anything of this kind. Perhaps they had more moderate appetites or better digestions than we have now.

There is a book of Indian origin called the Fables of Pilhay, or Bidpai, that may be found in our libraries, but is, I think, very little read amongst us. It was published in Sanscrit about the fifth century, under the title of "The Five Chapters." It is apparently a collection of popular anecdotes and fables, interspersed with state maxims and wise proverbs, strung together for a political or dynastic purpose. The design is, under the guise or reality of giving them good counsel, to exalt the authority of monarchs and the wisdom of prime ministers. It conveys the impression that no bad man can ever rise at court, and that female influence near the throne is always exerted on the side of innocence and virtue. The work is interesting to us because we see in it an instance of the means or representations by which the Indian people, who are sprung from the same race as ourselves, were soothed into voluntary submission to absolute authority. And it reminds us that this absolute authority, it matters not whether it was beneficially or tyrannically exercised, reduced the people of India to such a state of debility that they were overthrown by a handful of men of a nation congeneric with their own, but whose whole history has been and is a struggle for freedom. And it moreover teaches us that no material benefits that we can enforce on conquered India, no peace, no order, no civilization can for an instant compare with one breath of that freedom by inhaling which we have ourselves risen to greatness. The Fables of Bidpai were translated into Persian, Arabic, and, in the thirteenth century, into Latin. And now a most noticeable change took place in the reception of this work. In India, Persia, and Arabia it was accepted in good faith, and acquiesced in; but almost the moment it reached Europe, where the battle of liberty was being fought, it was replied to by one of the most grotesque parodies that ever was written, "The History of Reynard the Fox." This remarkable production, which is also a kind of collection of fables current at the time and place, chiefly Æsopian in cast, shows by overwhelming illustration that a simple undesigning man has not a chance of promotion at the court of an absolute ruler, that the most vicious, the meanest, and the craftiest knave is certain to rise to the place of chief favourite, and that the influence of the women about the court is always exercised on his behalf. Those two fable-epics, one emanating from the court, the other from the people, taken in conjunction with the Parable of Jotham and that of Agrippa, which may be said to have sprung from the same two sources, throw much light on the original purpose of fables, and on their interpretation generally. Their form fitted them naturally for the praise, or censure, or ridicule of rulers. The praise was made more pleasing by its indirectness, and by being thinly veiled, and was recommended to the multitude by some familiar comparison. The censure was rendered more biting by the same means, and also more popular. And in both cases the speaker or writer escaped the charge of being glaringly personal. If I desired to praise or to blame some great potentate, such as the Town Clerk or the Chairman of the Watch Committee, and if I were to describe those gentlemen by their names and titles, their modesty or their vanity might take offence, and your feelings towards them would blind you to the justice of my remarks; but if instead of "Town Clerk" or "Chairman" I were to say "Wolf" or "Ass," no offence could be taken, and you would be able to imbibe the moral in that calm, philosophical way that conduces to practical instruction. If one were to denounce and expose the conduct of great or rich men, it might be called factious and ill-natured, but if you compare them to lions, they take it as a compliment.

The lion and some other beasts agreed once on a time to go hunting together, and to divide the prey in common. They killed a stag, and divided it into four parts. But when they were about to take their several shares, the lion roared out: "The first part is mine because I am highest in dignity, the second is mine because I am strongest, the third is mine because I was most active in the hunt; and if you don't grant me the fourth part, there's an end to all friendship between us." This fable teaches us that when a rich or powerful man joins with persons of less wealth and influence in pursuing some enterprise, religious, or philanthropical, or political, he claims the whole control of it as his rightful due. That is what is called having the lion's share. In Church affairs he insists on the entire disposal of any patronage that is going. If he is one of the trustees of a vacant living, he says: "I claim one vote because my name is Dives, and a second because I have more influence than all of you put together, and a third because my contribution has been largest; and if you don't grant me the fourth you shall never enter my house again." So he has the appointment, and you can imagine the kind of man Dives will appoint. The same thing, I suppose, occurs among Nonconformists. Dives claims the whole management of the doctrine. You can imagine the kind of doctrine Dives likes. In politics, when various candidates are mentioned at an election time, the lion roars: "I claim the appointment first because I give most money to the cause, and, secondly, because, if you refuse, I'll have nothing more to say to you." Or perhaps he says: "This is bad weather for hunting; let us give our prey a holiday. If you don't agree with me you must go hunting by yourselves;" and somehow they are afraid to go by themselves, or they go in such small numbers that they have no chance of catching anything. Men speak contemptuously of woman's mode of reasoning. They say it consists in "Because I wish it." Now, the truth is, this is not reasoning at all, nor is it meant as such. It is merely the exercise of that power which woman has, and which we all must acknowledge, till she gets into Parliament. Most men are struggling all their lives to be able to say the same thing, to reason in the same way. Someone wrote a book on the "I wills" of Christ; I wish someone would write a book on the "I wills" of Dives. It might explain to us why it is that the "I wills" of Christ so often come to nothing. Now, nobody would venture to say all this directly and undisguisedly about rich men. It would be rude to do so. Therefore the fable-writers call them lions. I am only explaining what the fable-writers meant.

There may perhaps be some persons who think that the lion should be allowed his own way, and that it is black ingratitude to oppose him. They may think that the honour of being allowed to hunt in company with the royal animal is quite enough, without demanding any more in the division of the spoil than he chooses to give. For such persons there is a special fable ready

The lion, the ass, and the fox went hunting together. They took a good deal of game, and the ass was ordered to divide it. He divided it into three parts, and the lion tore him in pieces. The fox was then ordered to make the division, and he took a small portion for himself and gave all the rest to the lion. The lion commended him greatly, and asked him how he had acquired such correct notions of justice. "I learned them," said the fox, "from the fate of the ass." Here again you see how human conduct is ascribed to the ass and the fox in order to stamp it in the one case as foolish, and in the other as crafty. The ass does not go hunting with the lion. He prefers to hunt for thistles by himself, and in this he shows his good sense. Nor does the fox hunt in company with the lion. He, too, prefers to have all that he can catch as his own. It is man only who is so foolish as to go hunting in exalted society, and either to have nothing but the honour of the thing, or to be torn in pieces, or to get only a worthless fragment of the spoil. This last fable seems to shut us up to the alternative of being torn in pieces like the ass, or frightened into undue self-disparagement like the fox. But there is no need for going hunting with the lion at all. Fables only describe all kinds of human actions.

Wisdom is not to be learned from one fact or one fable, but from many facts and many fables. The wisdom we learn from these two fables is, if we wish to hunt in company, to hunt with our equals.

It is necessary to retain some knowledge of the political source from which the fable originally flowed, for without it we could trace no tide or current in the ocean of fabulous literature that time has accumulated. On the one side it confuses itself with the anecdote and the jest; on the other it blends into the tale, and the novel or romance. The use of the names of animals was never indispensable to fables, as we may see in Nathan's parable, and in some of the best of the fables known as Æsop's, as for instance, that of the old man who taught his sons the strength of union by showing how a bundle of sticks held together could not be broken; of the boy who was made to see the prudence of moderation by his inability to draw his hand, when full of filberts, out of a jar; the shepherd's boy who raised a false alarm of the wolf's coming so often that when the wolf really came his warning was not believed; and many others. Tales might be constructed within the limits of probability to inculcate or illustrate any line of conduct that the writer deemed important. Stories of this kind, when extended, become what we call novels. It is most probable that novels were originally fables, that is, tales illustrating morals or maxims, and that they in course of time sought to please only by variety of incident and beauty of style. Novels that depict human character, or that are written with a purpose, are long fables. Histories that modify or arrange facts so as to prove a theory are not prevented, by their being extended to eight or ten volumes, from belonging to the fabulous order. Some persons feel bound to countenance religious novels, because they suppose them supported by the example of the parables in Scripture. But a work of fiction proving or advancing religion, and religion illustrating some incidental topic by a fable or parable, are two different things. If all Scripture were a fable or parable, there would be a parallel between it and a religious novel, not otherwise. When we read a novel written to prove some social or political maxim, we say quite truly that, since all the facts are at the writer's disposal, another novel may be written to prove just the opposite. And the same thing may be said of a religious novel. But it could not be said of the teaching of Christ, or of Scripture generally. Fables were used extensively at one time, and, I believe, still are, for purposes of illustration in sermons. Specimens of those composed for that purpose may be found in old collections. A traveller vowed that he would give half of whatever he found to Mercury. He found a bag of dates and almonds. He ate the kernels of the almonds and the pulp of the dates, and gave the rest to Mercury. Men will try to cheat God when they get the habit of cheating each other. The devil once saw an old woman climbing up into a tree with her shoes on, and foresaw that she would fall and lay the blame on him. So he brought witnesses to the spot, and said to them: "You see that old woman getting up into a tree. Now, I know that she will fall, and I want you to bear witness that I did not persuade her to get up into the tree with her shoes on." Presently the old woman tumbled down, and when they asked her why she got into the tree without even taking off her shoes, she answered that the devil had driven her to do it. Then the devil brought his witnesses and proved that he was blameless in the matter. People, it would seem, had got so much into the way of throwing the blame on the devil of every foolish thing they did, that the devil, anxious, it may be, to prove that he is not so black as he is painted, found it necessary to provide machinery for defending his character and leaving us to bear the whole blame of our follies. A wicked man who had committed a great many villainies and escaped punishment, was again taken and imprisoned for a fresh offence. He besought the devil, who had so often helped him, to come to his assistance once more. The devil came to him carrying on his shoulders a great bundle of shoes with the soles worn away, and said to him: "My friend, I cannot help you any longer. I have been travelling up and down in so many places to get you out of your difficulties that I have worn out all these shoes, and I have no money left to buy others." This is a very familiar way of telling us that there are limits to the truth of the saying that the devil takes care of his own. A preacher or writer, standing on the history of the New Testament, may point his admonitions by stories or fables of this kind, but that, as I have said, is altogether different from building on the foundation of fiction a recommendation of truth. Under the head of fables of the kind of which I have been now speaking may be placed the following which I find in an old copy of Æsop. A woman had a drunken husband, and devised a scheme by which she thought she could terrify him out of his evil propensity. She took him one day, when dead drunk, and placed him in a burial vault, where she left him shut up until he had time to get sober and discover where he was. She then came and knocked at the door, and when he asked who was there, she answered that she was one who brought meat for the dead. "I don't want anything to eat," said he. "Bring me some drink." Another version of this story, which was composed to exemplify the ruling passion strong in death, has got into modern circulation, and most iniquitously a woman is made the heroine of it. I read it from a cutting out of some serial. It is called :—

"A Story with a Moral to it.

"About forty years ago a certain man, whose wife indulged rather freely in John Barleycorn, resolved to cure her of the disease. So he purchased a small jar of whisky, and also two coffins. The latter he stowed away in a corner of the house.

"On returning home from his employment as usual this day she was 'very far gone' indeed. He placed her in one coffin, and lay down in the other one himself. After a couple of hours the wife, no doubt rather uncomfortable, stretched out her arms and exclaimed :

"'Ugh! ugh! yah! Where am I?'

"Husband (in a disguised voice, most unearthly): 'You are dead, ma'am.'

"Wife: 'A'm dead; and are you dead, too?'

"Husband (still sepulchrally): 'Yes.'

"Wife: 'How long are you dead, sir?'

"Husband: 'A'm dead fourteen years.'

"Wife: 'And how long am I dead, sir?'

"Husband: 'You are seven years dead.'

"Wife: 'Well, God Almighty bless you, sir! You that's so well acquainted in this country, can you tell me where a'll get just half a glass of whisky?'

"We don't exactly remember what the moral is."

The people of the East conveyed instruction through the same channel. We find the following story in the life of Gautama, the founder of the Buddhist religion. There was a young woman who married early and had a child while still a girl. When her beautiful boy could run alone, he died. Her sorrow deprived her of reason for a time, and in her love for her dead child she carried it from house to house of her pitying friends, asking for medicine for it. A Buddhist convert sent her to Gautama. She went and said, "Lord and master, do you know any medicine that will be good for my child?" "Yes, I know of some," said the teacher. Now, it was the custom for patients to provide the herbs which the doctors required ; so she asked what herbs he would want. "I want some mustard-seed," he said ; and when the poor girl eagerly promised to bring some, he added : "You must get it from some house where no son, or husband, or parent, or slave, has died." "Very good," she said, and went to ask for it, still carrying her dead child with her. The people said, "Here is mustard-seed ; take it." But when she asked, "In my friend's house has any son died, or a husband, or a parent, or a slave?" they answered, "Lady! what is this that you say? The living are few, but the dead are many." Then she went to other houses ; but one said, "I have lost a son ;" another, "We have lost our parents ;" another, "I have lost my slave." At last, not being able to find a single house where no one had died, her mind began to clear, and, summoning up resolution, she left the dead body of her child in a forest, and returning to Gautama, paid him homage. He said to her: "Have you the mustard-seed?" "My lord," she replied, "I have not. The people tell me that the living are few, but the dead are many." Then he pointed out to her how the affliction from which she suffered was common to all ; thus her doubts were cleared, she accepted her lot, and became a disciple. The lesson which this apologue teaches, though infinitely below the Christian's hope, is yet one that the Christian need not despise. There is a selfish joy and a selfish sorrow which can only be allayed by merging them in the level waters of our common lot. An Eastern king, we also read, was unhappy from no definite cause, but simply that he was unhappy. His physicians advised him to wear the garment of a happy man. All his dominions were eagerly and carefully searched through, but no happy man could be found. The seed of this tale has taken a new form in modern dramatic literature. The prescribed garment was a shirt. After infinite pains, a happy man was found; but when negotiations were proposed for the purchase of his shirt, he showed a mysterious and determined opposition to part with the garment. As became the servants of an Oriental monarch, they used violence, and discovered that he wore a front. This was a good lesson to lay before a king.

It is only natural that fable should find a humorous outlet, and, having found it, should form a distinct channel. A miser sold all he had, and bought a wedge of gold, which he hid in the ground. Someone stole it, and when he lamented and tore his hair, a neighbour said to him: "Take a stone and put it where the gold was, and, seeing that you never would make any use of the gold, it will serve your purpose just as well." The wig of a bald man was blown off by a high wind. When his companions laughed, he answered that if the hairs that were born with him had left him it was no wonder that those which were not his own should go. A gnat stung a lion to madness, and went away singing a song of triumph. He then fell into a web, and was eaten up by a spider. This resembles the account of a man who fought with four men at a tavern, conquered them all, went home, and was thrashed by his wife. All the stories that we read in the newspapers about Mrs. Partington and Mr. Spoopendyke are fables.

This redundancy and promiscuousness into which fables run might be reduced to some order, it may be thought, by classification. A division into those with a moral and those without one seems an obvious course. But when we make the attempt we find that, in one sense of the word "moral," all fables have one, while in another sense none have it. All fables may be said to have a moral, because there is scarcely an incident in human life from which a lesson of some kind may not be drawn. When George IV. went to Edinburgh, Sir Walter Scott seized a wineglass from which his Majesty had just drunk, put it into his pocket, and vowed with enthusiastic loyalty that it should remain a priceless heirloom in his family for ever. He went home with the glass in his pocket, sat on it, and broke it. Franklin's stories of the "Whistle" and the "Grinding Stone" are instances of the wideness of the field from which worldly wisdom may be gathered. In this sense all fables have morals—that is, you may derive some knowledge of human nature from each of them. But if we take the word "moral" in its ethical meaning, very few fables possess one. Most fables merely aim at exposing some foible or variety of human character. Those that choose the most innocent and universal weakness are most popular. A fox, seeing some fine clusters of grapes on a vine, made several attempts to reach them, and failed. He went away, saying that they were sour and not fit to eat. There is nothing moral or immoral in depreciating what is unattainable; it is a harmless relief to disappointment. No one would blame me for saying how thankful I am that I was never made a bishop, since the moment a man becomes a bishop he is not fit for heaven nor earth. When a man attempts to get into the Town Council and fails, no one condemns him for congratulating himself on his failure to get into such a den of thieves. Or, on an election for the School Board, who would think of calling an unsuccessful candidate to account for blessing his stars that he was not sent to a place from which every honest Churchman runs away? The fox is the impersonation of shrewdness and prudence, and what he says must carry instruction. Solomon ate great quantities of grapes, and at the end he came to the conclusion that they were all sour, just as the fox did who ate none at all. There is great moral economy in coming to a just estimate of things and persons without going through the trial of many years' experience. We are ready to make a virtue of necessity. When things go contrary to our wishes, we say that was the very thing we wished. A huntsman bringing home a hare was overtaken by a horseman, who offered to relieve him of his burden by carrying it for him. The huntsman handed it to him, on which the other rode off as fast as he could. The huntsman, seeing his hare gone past hope, cried out after him: "You may have it; I make you a present of it." I once heard an anecdote which deserves to rank among fables. A man went into a chemist's shop and asked for some medicines, the price of which came to five shillings. When the parcel was ready he took it, and, laying fourpence on the counter, ran away. The chemist rushed to the door, but, seeing that the man was just about to turn a corner and escape, he cried out, holding up the fourpence: "You rascal! I have twopence by you still." Every beaten man looks for some particular in which he can say he had the best of the fight. A man invited a friend to an excellent supper. He had a dog, who also invited the friend's dog. When the invited dog saw all the good things, he began to wag his tail with joy; but when the cook saw him he seized him by the tail, whirled him round and round, and threw him out of the window. The dog, confounded at this treatment, limped away howling. Other dogs met him, and asked him whether he had supped very sumptuously. He, although he was almost fainting with pain, replied: "I drank so much wine that I scarcely know what way I came out." We all sympathize with that poor dog. He simply put on the best face he could under very humiliating circumstances. Why should he publish the inhospitality of the mansion and the cruelty of the cook to a censorious world? He lost his head as he was leaving the house, and he accounted for the accident in the way that should have been most appropriate under the circumstances. The fox who lost his tail, and would have persuaded all the other foxes to get rid of their tails as useless and burdensome encumbrances, was an animal of heroic enterprise. He might have got a false tail, but instead of this he boldly attempted to set the fashion of taillessness to universal foxdom. When we consider his daring ambition and the awkward character of the privation under which he suffered, we cannot help feeling pity for the wretched brute. If his misfortune had not been discovered until he had induced half a dozen other foxes to part with their brushes, it would be a relief to us. One now constantly thinks of him as shuffling and twisting and continually changing his seat in company, so as not to turn his back on anyone. He would ascribe this habit, no doubt, to natural politeness. There is no malice or unkindly spirit in those fables. We smile at the little vanities they expose, but it is with the consciousness that we are smiling at ourselves. There are other instances of a more serious import that we also recognize as universally applicable. An old man was toiling under a heavy load, and called on death to deliver him. Death appeared. "Ah!" said the old man, "I only wanted you to help me to carry this load." The fable of the dog in the manger, who could not eat the hay and would not let the cows eat it, we never apply to ourselves, because we always apply it in condemnation. The jackdaw who decked himself in borrowed plumes, the frog who wanted to make himself as large as an ox, and the ass who put on a lion's skin we regard with an ambiguous reserve. If we were to say what we feel, it would come to this: "I'm not so bad as that; if ever I did anything of the kind, I was not without good grounds for it, and I'll never do it again." There are fables that exhibit darker lines of character which we condemn without wholly disowning. A tunny-fish, pursued by a dolphin, leaped on land. The dolphin, in the eagerness of pursuit, also stranded himself. The tunny, seeing the dolphin gasping, said: "I can bear death, since I see the cause of my death dying with me." This characteristic is almost acknowledged as allowable by being undisguisedly ascribed to human beings. Two men at deadly enmity with each other sailed in the same ship. One sat at the prow, the other at the stern. A storm arose, and the vessel was about to sink. The man at the prow asked the pilot what part would sink first? The pilot answered, "The stern." "Then," said the man, "it will not trouble me to die, for I shall see my enemy die before me." If those fables were composed, as is most likely, in sympathy with the passion they indicate, it is another proof that the general purpose of fables is to describe, not to amend, our nature.

The maxim that necessity has no law is exhibited in a multitude of examples. A wolf, meeting a lamb going astray, said to him: "You insulted me last year." "Indeed," said the lamb, "I wasn't born then." "Then you feed on my pastures," said the wolf. "Good sir," said the lamb, "I have never tasted grass." "You drink at my well," said the wolf. "I assure you," answered the lamb, "my mother's milk is all I have ever drunk." "Well, I won't remain supperless," exclaimed the wolf, "even though you should refute all my charges;" and he ate him up. A cat got hold of a cock and accused him of being noisy, not letting folks sleep at night. The cock pleaded that he crowed at the wish of his owner, to rouse the labourers to their work. Then the cat said: "You are a wicked creature, because you have several wives." The cock replied that this was his master's fault, who wished to have as many eggs as possible. "You have many excuses," said the cat, "but I don't mean to fast;" so he devoured the cock. So it is in life: vain are the arguments of weakness. A hare argued out some point with a lion very eloquently. "What you say is very true," replied the lion, "but your arguments want teeth and claws." Alas for the lambs and cocks and hares! Sad is their fate—with, it may be, compensations—in the hard struggle for the survival of the fittest that goes on in savage nature. Sadder is their lot in this artificial state when they afford food and sport for man. But how saddest of all is it for their human counterparts, the real subjects of this parable, who must fill the maws of the hawks and wolves of society! No wolf ever charged a lamb with having insulted him. No lamb was ever buoyed up with the vain hope that a convincing reply would avert his fate. That preliminary torture is reserved for man. It is when the great nation goes to war with a weak one, or a great man goes to law with a small one, that the pretence of a just quarrel precedes the immolation. In these fables we must guard against making such allowances for the human being represented as the necessities of the beasts that represent them would demand. When the wolf or the cat says, "I cannot go without my supper," the argument is valid. Animals prey on each other, and there is no other limitation to the injury they do than their appetites. When we transfer the figure to men the case is quite altered. It is not for the gratification of his hunger or of any necessity of nature, but of his pride, his envy, his emulation, his vanity, that man devours his fellow-man. When Ahab wanted Naboth's vineyard and could not get it, "he laid him down upon his bed and turned away his face, and would eat no bread." That is the kind of hunger the human wolf endures. "The wicked sleep not except they have done mischief; and their sleep is taken away unless they cause some to fall." When we describe the wolf as endeavouring to pick a quarrel, we ascribe human attributes to him; and when we imagine the man whom he represents as suffering from hunger, we ascribe a wolfish appetite to him. But the necessities of the wolf do not justify the depredations of the man. The true state of the case is shown in another fable. A birdcatcher was about to sit down to a dinner of herbs, when a friend unexpectedly came in. He proceeded to kill a partridge which he had tamed for a decoy. The partridge begged for his life. "What would you do without me," he said, "when you spread your nets?" The birdcatcher spared his life, and determined to kill a fine young cock. The cock expostulated from his perch: "If you kill me, who will announce to you the appearance of dawn?" The man replied: "What you say is true; you are a capital bird at telling the time of day. But I and the friend who has just come in must have our dinners." Our real wants on earth are few. Man wants but little here below. When a man builds a palace, it is not for his own comfort, but for the admiration and envy of others. When he wears splendid garments, it is not to ensure warmth, but to attract attention. When he provides a luxurious banquet, it is not to satisfy his appetite, but to excel the banquet that has been given by somebody else. And to provide the means for doing these things he must make money by fair means or by foul. The social birdcatcher is willing to dine on herbs by himself, but when he has a friend to dine with him he must make a display, and he victimizes some unhappy client. Necessity has no law, it is true; but the necessities of human beasts are artificial, unreal, imaginary, vicious necessities—necessities of envy, hatred, and malice. We are fighting, not for food or raiment or houses, but for more expensive food, raiment, and houses than our neighbour can afford, and in order to obtain them we are ready to beggar our neighbour.

It must be again and again repeated that fables are wholly about men, and that the birds and beasts are mere *dramatis personæ*. One writer has said that it was unnatural to represent a fox wishing to eat grapes. Another has attempted to show the correctness of the imagery by referring to the expression in Solomon's Song (xi. 15): "The little foxes that spoil the vines." But even granting that Oriental foxes eat grapes, are they in the habit of calling them sour when they can't get them? An ass, having seen a lapdog jump on his master and get caressed by him, jumped on him in the same way and got beaten. The ass that would do such a thing would be a very uncommon ass. A Scotchman was once asked what he would do if an ass fell into a pit on the Sabbath-day. He cautiously answered that there was not in all Scotland an ass that was "sic an ass as to fall into a pit on the Sawbath-day." Animals, and human beings in relation to animals, are described as doing things they never do in order to represent how human beings act towards each other. No serpent would attempt to eat a file, nor would any man place a frozen serpent before his fire. No ass was ever such an ass as to put on a lion's skin; nor would any man carry an ass on a pole, as we read of in the fable of the man who wished to please everybody. No goose ever laid golden eggs, nor would any man be such a goose as to kill the bird that did lay them. A dog in a manger might object to having his slumbers disturbed, but it is possible the cows might dispute his right of possession. Indeed, a new version of this fable has lately appeared. A bull asked a dog lying on some hay to allow him to eat it. "No," said the dog; "it is my property." "Suppose we toss up for it?" said the bull, with anger in his eyes. "I never bet," said the dog, politely going away.

St. Paul, in interpreting an Old Testament figure, gives the true key for the interpretation of fables: "It is written in the law of Moses, Thou shalt not muzzle the mouth of the ox that treadeth out the corn. Doth God take care for oxen? or saith He it altogether for our sakes? For our sakes no doubt it is written" (1 Cor. ix. 9).

We may see the early application of fables to political purposes surviving largely in our present heterogeneous collections. No lesson is so frequently conveyed as the danger of change, and the wisdom of contentment. Some fish were being fried; they did not like the process, and jumped out of the frying-pan. They fell into the fire. An ass belonging to a gardener begged Jupiter to set another master over him. Jupiter gave him a bricklayer, who increased his burdens.

He prayed for a milder owner and got a tanner, who didn't spare even his skin. A tortoise, weary of crawling, wished to get into the air. An eagle took him up and let him fall on the rocks. A camel begged for horns like an ox. Jupiter denied his request, and, moreover, cut off his ears. The frogs asked for a king. Jupiter gave them a log. They were not content, so he gave them a heron, who devoured them daily. The oxen once were conspiring to destroy the butchers. One of them, old and experienced, said: These butchers know how to slaughter us scientifically and skilfully. If we get rid of them we shall only get into the hands of unskilful operators. The pigeons, terrified by the kite, asked for a hawk to defend them. When he came he killed more of them in a day than the kite would kill in a year. Such are the motives to contentment which our teachers favour us with: kites and frying-pans and butchers. A fox swimming over a stream was tormented by gnats. A swallow offered to drive them away. "No, don't," said the fox. "Those are cloyed with my blood. If a fresh hungry swarm came they would not leave a drop in my body." Moral: Never change the members of your Corporations or School Boards.

We can sometimes discern the political tendency of a fable by finding that there is another evidently intended to counteract its influence. A wolf saw some shepherds in a hut eating mutton. "Oh!" said he, "what a clamour you would make if you saw me doing that!" This insinuates that law-makers are law-breakers, and was written on the side of the wolf. Many a poor wolf, I dare say, shakes his head as he passes by the Town Hall. However, to save the law-breaking law-makers from falling into contempt another fable was written. A fox saw several old women eating a roasted hen. "Oh!" said he, "what an outcry and barking of dogs there would be if I were to do as you do!" "Thou base creature," answered one of the women, "we eat what is our own; you steal other's property." Shepherds and sheep always mean rulers and people in figurative language. To escape this association the fable of the old women and the hen was invented. But what does "the old women and the hen" mean? Of course it must have a figurative meaning, and must still represent rulers and people. It is not very complimentary to compare rulers to old women, but you and I are not accountable for it. The intention of the fable, therefore, is to impress such a conception of government as gives the ruler a right to devour the people. "We eat what is our own," said the old woman. A gentleman was telling me a little time ago that his father had been a member of the Corporation, and that in his days they were so scrupulous that they regarded the public money as if it were their own. "That is exactly what they do now," was my answer. In the same spirit the fable of the cock and the jewel has been violently perverted from its original purport. A cock scratching for food on a dunghill found a precious stone. "I would rather have a grain of corn," said he, "than all the jewels in the world." Obviously the cock means the husbandman of a nation tilling his fields. An attempt is made to dazzle him with stars and titles. "I can't live on glory," he answers; "I prefer wheat." To conceal this plain and striking presentment the following version of the fable was framed: A fresh young cock, in company with two or three pullets—his mistresses—raking upon a dunghill for something to entertain them with, happened to scratch up a jewel. He knew what it was well enough, but not knowing what to do with it endeavoured to cover his ignorance under a gay contempt. And finally, in the application, the jewel is taken to mean "virtue and learning," and the grain of corn "debauchery." In this way the fable is made to say the very reverse of what it was meant to say. And then, to prevent it from ever being rescued back to its true meaning, the following one was put in the place it used to occupy: An ass carrying a load of good provisions for his masters the reapers, met with a fine thistle, which he began to eat, saying: "Many epicures would think themselves happy if they had the delicate viands I now carry; but I prefer a thistle to them all." The high thinker, plain liver, and industrious toiler preferring solid fare for all the glitter and glory, is not like a cock choosing corn before jewels, but like an ass who prefers thistles to good provender. Even those fables that are celebrated and prized for the excellent advice they convey will be found, on examination, to be deficient in true moral teaching. A father who had quarrelsome sons taught them the value of union by showing that a bundle of sticks could not be broken taken together, but that each stick taken by itself could be broken easily. He then addressed them in these words: "My sons, if you are of one mind, and unite to assist each other, you will be like this bundle, uninjured by all the attacks of your enemies; but if you are divided among yourselves, you will be broken as easily as those sticks." This teaches that union is strength, but it does not touch on the use that is to be made of the strength, and there only it is that true morality comes in. There is scarcely such a thing as a fable, in our ordinary collections, of a high and ennobling tendency. The attempt even to introduce one has been resented. The general teaching of fables is that of the oak and the reeds. A large oak-tree was uprooted by the wind and thrown across a stream. It fell among some reeds, which it thus addressed: "I wonder how you, who are so light and weak, are not crushed by this strong wind?" They replied: "You fight with the wind, and consequently you are destroyed; while we bend before the least breath of air, and escape." No one could call this an elevating example. The prudence it inculcates is of the lowest kind—submit, and you are safe; and the analogy is not correct. The wind will blow just the same whether the oak or reed yields or resists. It is not so among men. The more the human reed bows his head, the fiercer will the human storm rage and oppress; the more the slave yields, the more the tyrant exacts. But, apart from prudence, there is the question of right and liberty. Is it not better in some cases to resist and be crushed than to submit and be secure? What would our condition be if our forefathers had never sacrificed themselves in contests where defeat for freedom was preferred to safety for slaves? Do we not owe all we most prize to uprooted oaks, and worse than nothing to reeds that came safe out of the tempest? Someone felt thoughts like these stirring in him as he read of the overturned oak, and he wrote the following fable: A willow challenged the oak to a trial of strength. A hurricane arose, when the pliant willow, bending from the blast, evaded all its force; while the generous oak, disdaining to give way, opposed its fury, and was torn up by the roots. Immediately the willow began to exult and to claim the victory, when the fallen oak interrupted his exultation: "Poor wretch! you owe your safety not to your strength, but to your weakness—not to your courage, but to your cowardice. I am an oak, though fallen; you are still a willow, though unhurt; and who except a mean wretch like yourself would prefer an ignominious life to the glory of meeting death in an honourable cause?" A writer on fable speaks of this one as "a travesty of a beautiful and well-known apologue, converting it into a lesson of false honour and foolish pride." There is another fable that carries the prudence of the reeds a step farther: A panther fell into a pit. The shepherds pelted him with stones; but some, moved with compassion, threw in some food to prolong his life. He got out of the pit, killed the shepherds who had attacked him, and slaughtered their herds with burning fury. Then those who had spared his life surrendered all they had, and begged only for their lives. The panther said to them: "I remember those who sought my life with stones, and those who gave me food. Lay aside your fears; I return as an enemy only to those who injured me." The moral is that when you see a tyrant down, if you help him up he will spare your life, and only ruin your neighbours; but if he were left in the pit, everyone would be safe. Some, however, prefer helping the panther and seeing others destroyed while they themselves are safe in slavery, to freedom and security for all. That is the reason why panthers exist on earth. A mouse seeing a kite caught in a snare, took compassion on him, gnawed the string that held him, and set him at liberty. The kite, the moment he was free, seized on the mouse and devoured him. An elderly philanthropic gentleman one day saw a little boy making strenuous but unavailing efforts to reach the knocker of a door. "Let me help you, my little man," said he, and he gave a loud knock. "Let us both run away now," said the little boy, "or we shall get licked." We must not conclude that every person whom we see striving to do something is deserving of help; and when a kite or a panther gets caught in a trap, the safest plan is to leave them there.

Fables, as I have already said, are pictures of life; and as a wide wisdom cannot be gathered from a single incident, no more can it from a single fable. One fable modifies the tenor by supplementing the history of another. A lion spared the life of a mouse, and the mouse afterwards gnawed asunder the rope by which some hunters had bound the lion to the ground. This story sets the mouse in the high position of being the benefactor of a lion, and surrounds him in consequence with temptations and dangers. There is another fable that tells what those dangers are. A lion, being caught in a net, entreated a mouse to gnaw the ropes and set him free, promising him all manner of rewards. The mouse complied, and as his reward asked for the lion's daughter in marriage. The lion gave his consent, but when they were returning home after the ceremony the bride inadvertently trod on her husband, and crushed him to pieces. Readers of the first fable might go away with the notion that all they had to do was to help some great man, marry his daughter, and live happy ever afterwards. So the second fable teaches that the young lady may put down her foot too forcibly some day.

In one case three fables are needed to tell all that should be known. A fisherman took a flute with him, and stood on a rock playing, supposing that he could coax the fish out of the water by his music. But when he found nothing could be done in that way, he laid his flute aside, cast in his net and caught a number of fishes. When he saw them dancing in the net, he said: "When I played you refused to dance, but now that I have caught you, you dance without music." This fable teaches that success is to be won only by work. We cannot do any thing great or good by the exercise of an idle taste. Industry and toil are necessary. Industry is so good a thing that, if a man had no need to seek an object in life, he should make an object for the sake of becoming industrious in striving for it. But there is something more than industry required. Sometimes it is said, in the pride of inexperience, that work must succeed, and that where there is poverty there must have been idleness and waste. This is not quite true. Success does not always wait on industry. The race is not always to the swift, nor the battle to the strong, nor wealth or fame to him who has painfully toiled for them. How many poets and painters fail to make themselves known!

Ah! who can tell how hard it is to climb
The steep where Fame's proud temple shines afar?
Ah! who can tell how many a soul sublime
Has felt the influence of malignant star,
And waged with Fortune an eternal war—
Check'd by the scoff of Pride, by Envy's frown,
And Poverty's unconquerable bar—
In life's low vale remote has pined alone,
Then drop'd into the grave, unpitied and unknown?

In our own neighbourhood how many die poor in proportion to those who become rich—although many of those who have failed toiled as assiduously as those who succeeded! Where lay the difference? In the absence of the "malignant star." In good fortune. This is indispensable to industry. We do not know what it is. It is beyond our reach and our conception. But without it Industry has not her full reward. We must not, therefore, pride ourselves on possessing the sure road to prosperity, or on having success under our control. A man going to law should have, it is said, not only a good lawyer, and a good jury, and a good judge, and a good cause, but also good luck. The second fable teaches us how good fortune may accomplish what work and skill fail in doing. Some fishermen, wearied with fishing and spent with hunger and grief because they had taken nothing, resolved to return home in despair. But, behold, as they were about to depart, a fish—that fled from another that pursued it—leaped into the boat. The fishermen brought it to the city, and sold it at a great price. But do those two fables exhaust the vicissitudes of human history? May not a time come when industry will fail and fortune forsake us? What then remains? There is a third fable that answers the question. Some fishermen dragged a net in the sea, which when they felt it to be very heavy, they were filled with joy, supposing it contained a great quantity of fish. But when they drew it to the land and found that it contained only a large stone, they were oppressed with sadness. One of them, a very old man, said to his fellows: "Set your hearts at ease: for Sorrow is the sister of Mirth. One ought to foresee changes that are likely to befall, and in order that he may be able to bear them more easily when they come, he ought to persuade himself that they will come." This fable, the "moral" says, signifieth that he that remembereth man's condition is not daunted by adversity. What remains, then, when industry and fortune fail? Ourselves. We are above the slights of justice and the strokes of fortune. A time will inevitably come when all outer things will fail us. Nay, many times come in the course of our lives when our efforts seem vanity and our hope a false light that brought us on the rocks, and our faith a broken reed piercing our hand. Some men then give way to despair, and fall into low ways of thought, mistaking the importance of the occasion. Those times of apparent loss are only times of trial. They prove whether we have really lost or won in the battle of life. The loss of money, fame, friends, is no essential loss. The only essential loss is the loss of our own love for God and man. The affairs of the world are not ends, but means to an end. That end may be gained whether things go well or ill with us. All the laws of natural cause and effect are subservient to that greater moral law by which fortitude is strengthened and trust in righteousness deepened. It is well to play our part and fight our battle nobly and manfully in earthly affairs. It is well for this reason—that we shall find one day that the things about which we fought, and the field on which we struggled, were shadows, and that the soul, made pure and strong in the encounter, is itself the victory and the everlasting prize.

FROM LANCASHIRE TO LAND'S END.

I FIND some difficulty in explaining to my own satisfaction why I went to Cornwall in the spring of this year (1882). It was partly the alternative to another journey which was impossible. An Irishman's conventional mode of accounting for his absence from Ireland in times of trouble was that he left the country "for a reason he had." I did not go to Ireland for a reason my wife had. We resolved to go to Cornwall instead. The remembrance of an old tradition that identified the populations of Ireland and Cornwall by common origin, or conquest, or immigration, pointed the way to this resolve. Referring to Black's "Guide-Book to Penzance," our farthest Cornish destination, I learned that the soil is noted for its extraordinary fertility, and especially for its growth of potatoes. This confirmed both the tradition and our purpose. The people had evidently disciplined the land into congenial productiveness. While speculating on this subject, the Manchester newspapers suddenly burst into a blaze of descriptions of riots that were raging at Cambourne between the earlier and later inhabitants of the district. Streets were said to be desolated, chapels wrecked, innumerable heads broken. There was no more room for doubt. We started on our journey. We took with us Black's "Guide," a novel by a celebrated lady romancist, said to be eloquent on Cornish scenery, and a book by an author named Bradshaw, who, I was informed, was a great authority in that line. As I consulted those writers promiscuously, it is possible I may confound their remarks with each other's or with my own.

We took tickets for Plymouth, intending to spend a day or two there on the way and see what was to be seen. A fellow-traveller said, in a commonplace kind of way, that it always rained at Plymouth. Having ultimately come from Manchester, where it is always said to rain, and penultimately from Killarney, where it is also said always to rain, I began to ask myself what was to be gained by travelling. When we reached Plymouth it became clear to me that there is variety even in rain, and that although Killarney, Manchester, and Plymouth may, in this respect, be very much alike, yet Plymouth was like Manchester and Killarney put together. When I say that this was clear to me, I mean to imply that nothing else was clear. It certainly did rain at Plymouth. Cabs and ships and men were moving, but they were like shadowy ghosts, half visible in rainy darkness. The rain was the one substantial visitant from the upper world. The hotel we went to was chosen for the fine view it was said to afford. It fully answered its engagement. If anyone desires to have an unequalled view of rain I should advise him to go there. Some blurred objects were pointed out, said to be a lighthouse and a breakwater. They may have been—it was impossible to deny anything that might be said of them—but their occupation was gone, or reversed. When I got up the next morning I found it, like a giant refreshed with sleep, raining with renewed vigour. When a man's pleasures fail him, he has his necessities to fall back upon. Breakfasting is a necessity. The waiter informed me that they had some fine whiting, caught that morning. I sympathized deeply with them. We differed only by an accident. They were caught out of the wet, I into it—"in" and "out" are only accidents.

The Tamar separates Devon from Cornwall. It

is crossed near Plymouth by a suspension-bridge that spans the valley at a fearful height. There is no need to linger on this bridge. When we get into Cornwall we shall have to cross the bridges very slowly, because, being made of timber, now in a state of partial decay, if the train caused any considerable commotion, they would give way and precipitate the passengers to a depth of some hundred or more feet. On inquiring why we always went over the bridges at so leisurely a pace, it was encouraging to have this reason assigned; though it had rather an Irish flavour about it, and reminded one of the old woman who having crossed a bridge, and finding it marked "dangerous" on the other side, ran back as fast as she could. The bridge over the Tamar at Saltash is an iron one; therefore we may pass it over quickly. There is another reason for avoiding local details, which I may as well mention. No object in Cornwall that I have seen resembled the written or pictorial descriptions of it. There are numerous illustrations of the same rocks or castle which are as unlike to each other as to the original. Travellers seem to think that they will not be believed unless they give accurate measurements and minute particulars. My opinion is that the more general the description the more likely it is to be true and to be believed. There is no tradition in Cornwall so universal—so *semper ubique et ab omnibus*—as that Christianity was planted in the country by a multitude of saints, male and female, who came from Ireland. While this statement was left to its own probability, and to established opinion, it was safe enough. Unfortunately the Cornish people were not satisfied with generalities. They wanted to be exact and to supply evidences. So they point out a huge rock of granite, with a hollow in one side, that happens to lie conveniently by the margin of the water, and assert that it is the actual boat in which one of those missionaries crossed the sea. It must, however, be said that this story corroborates, by its imaginative character, the tradition which it fails to make good by material proof. It is precisely of the same kind as the tales of wonder that are prevalent among the Irish peasantry. I well remember an old ruined church which was said to have been transported one night from a distant part of the country to the spot where it then stood. A large rock in a river that lay between its two sites was always referred to as evidence of the fact, it being a foundation-stone that dropped from the edifice while *in transitu*. It must not be supposed that these stories are or were really credited by the peasantry. They were regarded just as the labours of Hercules were by an ancient Greek. They were believed by the imagination in order to be smiled at by the reason. We all believe, or realize to a certain extent, the wildest fiction that we read, in order that we may extract the desired pleasure from it, which otherwise we could not possibly do. A peasant, one evening at Trevena, showed me two distant spots eight or ten miles asunder, which measured the single step of a giant on some emergency, just in the same humorous way in which I have heard the nocturnal flight of the church described to me in my boyhood. We too often misconceive and undervalue the true nature of those popular fables. They are the first human recoil from the mechanical realities of mere animal life. It might be expected that this imaginative faculty would produce a greater number of poets than either Cornwall or Ireland can lay claim to. Imagination, when circumstances are favourable, produces poetry; but when circumstances are not favourable it has other, and, for the time, much better work to do. It is the soil from which religious feeling springs, and it stimulates to ceaseless personal adventure. "Emigration," says a very able essayist in Cornwall, "has been so large of late years as to keep the population almost stationary, . . . in all parts of the world, in North and South America and Australia, knots of Cornish emigrants will be found—generally prosperous, though more through speculative qualities than the cool and thrifty determination of the sons of the North."* This description applies generally to Irish emigrants. "Their impulses, tastes, and pleasures," this same writer says, "are almost all gregarious. In old days they met, quarrelled, and fraternized in faction fights like those of Ireland, wrestling matches, hurling matches, and similar amusements. The gentry seemed to have lived in a social Castle Rackrent kind of fashion of their own." "The manners and habits of the Cornish populace before the time of Wesley," we again read, "seem to have strongly resembled those of the Irish, without the religious fervour which characterized the latter. There were the same clannish propensities, the same faction fights, the same riotous fairs and noisy funerals, the same disposition for turbulent encounters with the established authorities on every local occasion." "I saw, in some poor cottages," another writer says, "little girls barefooted and with their hair

* Herman Merivale.

floating in disorder down their backs, who reminded one of Ireland." Every writer on Cornwall unconsciously testifies to this similarity. The habit of piling the sheaves of corn in stacks of an intermediate size before they are finally stacked in the hay-yard—which I heard an Englishman ridicule in Ireland as a proof of ignorance and indolence—prevails through Cornwall, where it is accounted for by visitors as a provision against the damp and uncertainty of the climate. The phenomenon of red sheep—the result of an artificial process for a sanitary purpose—is common, and, I think, peculiar to both countries. All the superstitious omens of evil, such as the croaking of a raven, seeing a magpie, breaking a looking-glass, the howling of dogs, whistling by night, are the same. The Cornish motto "one and all" is paralleled by the Irish one *sheen fane*—"ourselves alone," although the description given of one of the two peoples, the Cornish, will equally suit the other: "Never was a small people more curiously and readily divisible into factions, or more disinclined to really useful co-operation."

The people of Cornwall were devoted Catholics till the Reformation, when they fought hard for the old religion. A foreign creed was, however, forced on them, and then was noticeable the want of religious fervour which has been mentioned. We can scarcely be surprised at it when we recall one or two of the current clerical anecdotes of the time. It is stated as a fact that, a wreck happening on a Sunday morning, the clerk announced to the assembled parishioners "That measter would gee them a holladay." On another occasion, it is said, news arrived of a wreck during the service. The congregation started up. "Stop," cried the minister, in a loud voice. The people looked at him in surprise while he divested himself of his robes, and rushed down among them. "Now," said he, "let us start fair," as he led the way to the wreck. At Kenwyn two dogs, one of which was the parson's, were fighting at the west end of the church; the parson, who was reading the second lesson, rushed from his desk and parted them. On his return, not remembering where he had left off, he asked the clerk, "Roger, where was I?" "Why, doon parting the dogs, measter," said Roger. This was the time when a man of some position in society was said to have driven an ass at night, with its leg tied up and a lantern round its neck, along the summit of a high cliff, that the halting motion of the animal might resemble the plunging of a vessel under sail, and thus tempt ships to run in, as if there was sea-room. Wesley paid his first visit to Cornwall in 1743, and restored to the people a religion of their own, and a channel for the zeal of their race.

It is only fair to note one or two facts that distinguish the history of Cornwall from that of Ireland. The Saxons did not push their way beyond a line running transversely from Plymouth to Tintagel. The Cornish people have, therefore, a claim to descent from their very ancient King Arthur, whoever he was. In the next place, the Normans never established themselves firmly in Cornwall. Great names and titles vanish there like mists from the sea. This fact has passed into a superstition. A third heir is scarcely known; a fourth never. One cause of this constant change was the frequent occurrence of family tragedies and premature deaths. There are several instances of great landowners being compelled to sell their property in order to bribe courtiers to procure a pardon for them when lying under sentence of death for murder. Aristocratic influences are consequently weak, and Methodist teachers and mining captains are the counsellors and leaders of the people by a natural and undisputed right. The population of Cornwall, again, at least some twenty thousand of them, work under ground, where cattle cannot be made their substitutes. The mining interest dominates the political economy of Cornwall, and is fed by constant supplies from the great speculation field of London.

Having lingered beyond intention on the Saltash bridge, we must at all peril speed over the others. The country shows more and more the signs of mining operations as we advance. The earth looks as if it were being turned inside out. Towards Cambourne we seem to be steaming through an uneven sea of mud. About this place, probably from the monotony of the scene, I fell into a doze and began to dream. I fancied that three fresh passengers entered the carriage. They soon began to talk about the Irish riots. "Irish has nothing to do with it," said one who seemed to be an inhabitant of the place; "one chap met some ill-treatment and resented it, and the quarrel spread. That was the sum and substance of the matter. English and Irish were pure accidents." "Who would ever hear anything like that, except in a dream!" thought I to myself. "Don't you think it was a national quarrel, then?" asked another of the party. "Of course it became national when two nations took it up and made it their own, and blew the trumpets of five hundred newspapers to inflame it," answered the first speaker. "It blazed and burned in the air of nationality, whereas it would have died out, smothered in the narrowness of personal anger, if let alone. Look at two armies destroying each other—or, as we call it, waging glorious war on each other. Forget that they are French and Germans, and you will see that they are simply murderers. Renew the idea of their distinct nationality, and murder becomes glory." "What extraordinary things dreams are!" was my mental exclamation. "But did not an Irishman begin it?" said the questioner. "The man who began it, or on whose act it first gained notice, was not an Irishman," was the reply, "though he was the son of Irish parents. He thought he was wronged, and I believe he was, and he looked for redress. Then the differences of country, which had nothing whatever to do with the rights of the question, were dragged in." Here the train stopped at a station with a sudden shock, which I expected would wake me up. But to my astonishment it did not. In fact, without being aware of it, I had been awake the whole time. The scene was real.

Penzance takes its name from a projecting head of land on which a little chapel of St. Anthony stands. It is therefore called Penzance, which means Holy head. The accent in Cornish names marks the adjectival syllable. San is holy, Pen, héad. So the pronunciation is Penzánce. The town takes the head of John the Baptist for its arms. The little town of Marazion, or Marketjew, stands opposite to St. Michael's Mount, within a few miles of Penzance. The sound of the name has given occasion to the supposition that the Jews traded largely there. Their ancient fondness for tin renders it probable that they may have done so, but if they did, the fact has no connection with the name. Marghas means a market, Ian is the adjective of island. Marazion means Island market, so called from the proximity of Michael's Mount, which is an island. Marghasjew, or as it is now called Marketjew, signifies Thursday-market. A street in Penzance is so called.

I went out to have a stroll by moonlight along the seaside at Penzance. Any description of this scene would be only an attempt to describe one's own feelings, and they cannot be described. Suffice it to say that the lights shone in heaven and the sea murmured on earth. I saw another light—a gaslight—on the opposite side, and heard a murmur of human voices. One may linger too long asking, "What are the wild waves saying?"

15

I went across the road, and found myself one of a thick crowd under an immense tent, at one end of which stood a platform hung round with a miscellaneous assortment of articles for sale. A young man stood on the platform with a tin teapot in his hand. "Ladies and gentlemen," said he, "this teapot is the only one left of three thousand that I have sold within the last couple of days. It is made of the strongest Cornish tin. An old lady bought one of them and put it on the hob. The cover began to move up and down. She laid her hand on it to keep it still. It went on moving. She sat on it, but it resisted her efforts. She had two lodgers, navvies. One of them sat on it with her, but the cover never stopped moving. The other lodger sat with them. It burst. The old woman and a tomcat were blown up the chimney and the two navvies have not been heard of since. You'll say," he concluded, "that this is a great lie—but—it *is*." One or two of the crowd tried to meet his style in kind by chaffing him. "Ah," said he, "wherever there's light you are sure to have moths fluttering about it."

Between Penzance and the Land's End on the coast is the Logan stone. Antiquaries insist that it should be called the logging stone; to log meaning to sway or oscillate. Wilkie Collins gives a description of it, and also a picture. The description I will quote. I rejoice that I can't quote the picture. "This far-famed rock rises on the top of a bold promontory of granite, jutting far out into the sea; split into the wildest forms, and towering precipitously to a height of a hundred feet. When you reach Logan stone, after some little climbing up perilous-looking places, you see a solid, irregular mass of granite, which is computed to weigh eighty-five tons, resting by its centre only, on a flat, broad rock, which in its turn rests on several others stretching out around it on all sides." The picture confirms this account, representing the stone as being on the top of the pile of rocks. If a mere historian: someone who only wrote histories, and did not know the difference between fact and fiction—like Froude or Macaulay—wrote after this fashion you could not blame him. But when an habitual writer of fiction—if Mr. W. Wilkie Collins be *the* Wilkie Collins—who ought to be able to distinguish fact when he saw it from fable, makes things appear as they are not, our condemnation must be without extenuating circumstances. I will never say how many feet high a rock or castle is, nor how many tons a stone weighs, nor how far distant one spot is from another. If I made the attempt, I should most probably be quite as wrong as others; and if I were right, no one would be able to form an idea of these things, or feel an interest in them more than before. It is the human foot-race that invests the sand with absorbing and mysterious interest. It is the relic of human life—the indentations that rage and fear and death have made on the earth that arrest our sympathies. The Logan stone is not twenty feet from the ground—be the same more or less—and so far from being on the summit, the pile of rocks rises to a great height behind it, quite hiding it from the sea. This pile was, in fact, a keep or fortress at some extremely remote period. It is known as Trereen Castle. Either a castle stood there or the rocks were made to fulfil the defensive functions of a castle. The promontory widens inwards from the sea, and was protected by three lines of circumvallation; one at the neck of the rocky pile, another where the promontory first juts out from the main shore, and a third between those two. The moment the guide called my attention to those ancient fortifications, I regarded the Logan stone only in a secondary way. Thoughts of the fierce struggles that raged on the spot, and of the strange men who engaged in them, thronged my imagination. Yet the Logan stone must have been there also. Were those bold warriors acquainted with its peculiar property? When did its power of vibration commence? Who first made the discovery? The great capabilities of successful defence which the place naturally presented had no doubt led to its being chosen by some piratical invader as a fortress from which he could pillage the surrounding country, and, at last, if necessary, escape in his ships. It was not likely that he troubled his head about the Logan stone, even enough to make mistakes about it, as Mr. Wilkie Collins did. I asked the guide if there were any record or tradition as to the time when the stone was first observed to be capable of motion; and he repeated, in reply, a long legendary tale, a few sentences of which I wrote down afterwards from memory. "Calm was the eve by Trereen shore. The sun, a ball of red, hung on the margin of the sky. His beams gently heaved like sleeping sea-birds on the waves. The air was still. But fierce rolled the tides of battle to and fro before the rocky home of Cathmor. He had wooed the daughter of Clougal, chief of the Glen. But the maiden turned from his love. 'Leader of men,' she said, 'seek elsewhere a heart that can beat to thine. The halls of chiefs welcome thy coming, and distant isles are close to thy fast-sailing ships. Isola's love is given to another.' Darkness gathered on Cathmor's brow as when the blast from the mountains settles on the lake. He went in silence. But he came suddenly with his warriors and bore off the shrieking maid. Her friends raised the cry of war through the valley. They poured forth as the stream rushes over rocky falls and shouts in its torrent joy. At the last rampart they joined in fight. They struggled to and fro as the trees of the forest mingle their branches in the fury of the tempest. Cathmor gained his home of rocks. He was seen on the craggy pile. Isola stood by his side. Her hair hung loose. The sunbeams sparkled in its golden mazes. The tear was in her eye, as the dew on the lonely flower that hangs on the cliff. With one hand she sheltered her eyes from the sun as she gazed through her tears on her brothers. 'Cathmor,' shouted Clougal, 'restore the daughter to her sire, the maid to her lover. Let there be peace. We will gladly see thy ships returning when thou sailest over the dark waves.' 'Cathmor yields not to man,' cried the haughty chief. 'When the rock on which she leans shall move at the pressure of Isola's hand Cathmor will yield.' Isola's heart beat high at Cathmor's words. She stood in the pride of her maiden strength. She pressed her white hand, and the rock heaved to the tremor of her touch. Loud and long rose the shout of wonder and joy. 'Strong is the rock,' said the sea-borne chief, 'and stronger is love; but more steadfast than the rock and stronger than love is the pledged word of Cathmor. Let the maid depart. Time will lessen the pain of Cathmor's heart. Let there be peace.' Calm was the eve on Trereen shore."

I asked the guide where he got the legend. He heard a gentleman read it, he said, out of a small, square book, printed on thin paper, and full of lines and figures which he could not understand. "Was Bradshaw the name?" I asked. He said he thought it was.

On our way to Land's End—we drove in a car drawn by a single horse, I must observe—we came upon a donkey lying on the middle of the road. As we came near the animal turned his head and looked at us languidly, then resumed his former attitude and lay still. The driver made a circuit, and left him undisturbed. We were followed by another carriage containing a more numerous party, and drawn by two horses. We watched with some curiosity to see what would happen. The moment the donkey saw a carriage and pair approaching he arose, shook his ears deferentially, and walked aside with instinctive recognition of greatness. I could note the gleam of assured triumph that passed over the features of the occupants of the two-horse carriage at the donkey's homage. It was a subject of thought for me during the rest of the day, and for many days. Why do people ride in two and four and six horse carriages? Because they expect to meet donkeys. Why do men spend their lives in making money which they never spend? For the sake of the donkeys. Why do statesmen soar beyond their modest practical duties and embroil the nations in strife? That donkeys may rise at their approach. Why do town councillors make orations about ship canals? Why do people wish to get on school boards? That donkeys who would not move for them before may bow their ears for them as they pass by. Why do young men smoke cigars? To astonish donkeys. What is all extravagant taste in art and dress for? For donkeys. The lesson that I learned at the Land's End made me a wiser, without being a sadder man. I constantly think of that donkey. My wife says that I am growing very careless about my appearance and wearing shabby clothes. A friend with whom I was about to take a walk the other day somewhat too considerately suggested that I should put on an overcoat. He was looking at my old jacket as he spoke. I knew what he meant, but I had not gone to the Land's End for nothing. If he chose to lie on the road while I passed let him do so. There is much more time lost in waiting for a donkey to rise than there is in going round him. When I began to prepare this paper last week, I said to myself with emphatic warning, "Mind that you do not attempt to drive in a carriage-and-pair style before the Literary Club. There are no donkeys there."

The Land's End is a place to sit quietly at and think and feel. The feelings created by such scenes are rich with the uncoined ore of humanity—why should we mingle them with the alloy of conventionality to make them circulate? They are flooded with the milk of human kindness—why churn this milk into words that retain no life, and never can become emotion again? The thought of the Land's End, and the question that arises as the eye scans the distant sweep of ocean—what lies beyond?—are the chief ingredients of the mood that the locality begets. But when we begin to philosophize we know that America lies beyond, and that if our thoughts only continue to travel they will come round to the very point from which they started, and the Land's End becomes the end of romance. Let us make-believe that the world is flat.

In a field by the roadside, not far from Penzance, stands a circle of tall gray stones, nineteen in number. How they were brought there or where from is a perplexing inquiry. There are no such stones anywhere near, and if there were it is difficult to comprehend how they could be conveyed to this spot and set erect. They are called the Nineteen Merry Maidens. Again I say—be the same more or less. I counted them several times, but I do not pledge myself to their exact number. I measured the distance between them, and the diameter and the circumference of the circle, but I was no wiser. At night I read their true history in one of the books which I had brought with me—which of them I am unable to say.

It was in the days when the ancient Druidic worship was yielding before the mild doctrine of the true religion. But the later germs of truth lay yet unfolded in the stern soil, and the habits of a gloomy ritual lingered in the first beams of the growing dawn. A group of maidens from Penzance, forgetting or heedless that it was the Sabbath Day, went to join in their accustomed dance in the field of meeting. The Christian priest, who had previously been a Druid, and was now fired with new-born zeal, hurried after them to prevent the profanation. He found them standing in a ring, just about to commence the measure, and entreated them to forbear. The wilful maidens could not understand why their usual pastime should be abandoned. They ridiculed his scruples. The priest changed his entreaties to threatenings. "Gladsys Pentreath," said he, addressing the ringleader of the party, the fairest and the merriest of the daughters of Penzance, "wilt thou dance on the day of holy rest—on the Sabbath Day?" "We are ready to dance for a whole week of Sabbath Days," said the laughing girl, as she extended her arms to her companions on each side to commence the movement. "Remain where you are," said the angry priest, "until a week of Sabbaths comes and closes, and be a warning to future time that the laws of religion cannot be broken with impunity." Just in the circle in which they stood the maidens were changed into stone, and there they remain rooted in the earth to the present day. Strangers long felt an unaccountable sadness grow on their spirits as they looked on the group, not knowing the strange fact of their transformation. An air of sullen terror struggling with defiance breathed from the petrified forms. The attitudes of the graceful maidens, as they were just about to sweep round in undulating motion, contrasted in some felt but unintelligible manner with the fixed and motionless figures of the stones. No sunshine ever seemed to gladden the spot. A rebellious darkness that appeared to come from within lowered on the granite masses, and repelled the fondling and comforting daybeams.

After many centuries had passed away, and partial stagnation had long succeeded the first glad influx of Christianity, a fresh wave of life, welling from a distant source, swept over the land. The whole population hastened to bathe in its water, and renewed their dying love. For a time all the usual occupations of daily life were forsaken, and frequent religious services succeeded each other almost without intermission. The church-bells pealed day after day for a whole week—morning and evening the summons to prayer rang through the parish from the church-tower, and was answered by thronging crowds. On Saturday morning the call to worship was repeated and responded to. In the evening again the bell pealed its invitation, and the whole cycle of a week of Sabbaths was almost completed.

The bell rang loud, and the congregation gathered. The bell ceased to ring, and the people sat in expectant silence, but no clergyman appeared. They waited for a long time in surprise, and at last departed in angry unrefreshment.

The clergyman was a stranger who had exchanged duties with the resident pastor during the mission. During his stay he had formed an attachment to the daughter of a farmer in the neighbourhood. They had fallen into the habit of going to the church together for some days, and the girl had promised, when they met on Saturday evening, in the field of the Nineteen Merry Maidens, to give a final answer to his offer of love. Just as the bells began to ring she entered the field. It appeared quite strange to her—no merry maidens were there! Astonished, and concluding that she had mistaken the entrance, she passed on to the next field, thinking it must be the one she sought. But this field, too, was empty. Excited and reft of all self-possession, she hastened on, and passed from field to field and lost herself in the wild and fruitless search. Her lover came at the appointed hour. He had yet time to receive the promise that was to make his life happy, and then proceed with his affianced bride to the service that was to conclude his engagement. He, too, entered the field, and seeing no circle of stone pillars, hastily took for granted that he had mistaken the place in his eagerness, and immediately directed his steps to the adjoining field just as the object of his search passed from it at the opposite side. Surprised and confounded at finding this also without the tokens that distinguished the appointed trysting-place, he lost all sense of time and sound. The beating of his heart was louder than the peal of the bell. For hours he continued his pursuit, and during the whole time, the affrighted girl left each field just as he entered it.

That night the inhabitants of Penzance were disturbed by strange sounds heard in the streets. Some of them rose and went to the windows to ascertain from what source they proceeded. By the light of the clear moon they saw a number of girls in strange attire, and speaking an unknown language, wandering through the streets. They uttered exclamations of grief and astonishment as they approached house after house and failed apparently to discover what they expected to find. Their eager words began to subside into stifled moans and despairing wails, when a sudden cry from one of them caught the attention of all the others. They flocked together to the place from which the cry came, and a simultaneous exclamation of joy burst from every lip as they recognised the ancient cross that stood by the market-house—the only object in the town, as it would seem, that was familiar to them. A solemn silence succeeded to this burst of glad recognition. They knelt in a cluster round the old cross, and as the wondering watchers gazed, they slowly faded from view.

The next morning the merry maidens were in their usual place. But observers ever afterwards noticed a change in their appearance. The gloom and the shadow had departed, and when the sun poured his beams on the gray stones, no longer repelling his sympathy, they basked in the grateful warmth and reflected his brightness.

We returned towards the south by train to Falmouth, and travelled by water to Truro, through a succession of wooded lakes that opened before us and closed behind us as we went.

There is no railway further than Bodmin on the way to Tintagel. A distance of some twenty miles must be walked or driven over. The road is said to be the most dreary and uninteresting that can be found. Fortunately we did not learn this until after we had made the journey. No feature of what is generally considered fine scenery presented itself. Neither lake, wood, nor castle embellished the view. But we had near and distant objects to contemplate. We passed alternately between steep and sloping banks, covered with flowers, that shut out the landscape, and low hedges that allowed the horizon to be seen. Wide sweeps of undulating hill that gathered afar off into the semblance of endless plains, and melted insensibly into the low-lying heavens, carried away the thought till it lost its distinctness and became a mysterious emotion, resembling the remote objects in the scene where mountain-tops and clouds were indistinguishable. Bold and craggy eminences at another time drew the mind into their likeness, and inspired the mood that dares and defies the blows of man or fortune. Again, tall hills lifted the soul to the height where, in ambitious reveries, the holiness of earth is forgotten. Then we suddenly drove into ravines of blossoming hyacinths, that called our attention to the immediate products of Nature, and compelled us to listen to her low and soothing voice. "Come," she said, "to my bosom, and learn to contemplate the modest beauties that are life's daily bread. They are always at hand; they will never fail, never deceive. Enlarge your imagination, if you will, with the indistinct forms of cloudland, but forget not the tenderness of home and friendship, and the sweetness and fragrance that glorify the near and narrow way." The driver directed our attention to two savage crags that thrust themselves forward and frowned at each other across a deep valley. This, we were told, was called the Devil's Jump. There are two divergent traditions about the devil in Cornwall. The Cornish housewives are famous for the excellence and varied contents of their pies. There is no conceivable thing that may be eaten, or that can be thought possible to be eaten, that they do not dress in this kind of dish. Having subdued one world to their culinary enterprise, they aspire to other worlds, and openly express their desire to catch the devil and cook him in a pie. The devil has heard of this, and he keeps out of the way. It is said that he never dares to make his appearance in Cornwall. But, on the other hand, there are various localities that testify to his visits by their names. There are devil's pits, and coits, and caldrons, and heights, and hollows, just as in other places. The explanation of those contradictory evidences is that the devil does visit Cornwall, but that he is very much on his guard, hiding behind bushes and rocks, and never venturing into the haunts of fashion and parading the streets as he does in other places. He skulks about in a cowardly manner, and acts more like a poacher than a licensed sportsman. Once, on a summer's eve, a youth and a maiden wandered in a path that leads near one of these crags. The balmy air trilled to the song of the thrush. The streamlet sparkled and sang light-heartedly as it sped from its cradle in the moors to its final home in the ocean. No pollution of town or factory clogged the liquid clearness of its rippling melody. It was pure as the hearts of the youthful pair who drew nigh. The devil happened to be lurking somewhere near, and he immediately crept out and stationed himself on the crag and lay down to listen to what the lovers were saying. Listeners seldom hear good of themselves. "Neelah," said the youth, "do not postpone our happiness through excessive prudence. I am strong and healthy: you shall never want something to put into the pie, though I were to seize the arch fiend himself." The devil sprang up in consternation, jumped across the chasm and disappeared, leaving his name to the locality, and confirming the pious disposition of the Cornish people.

Passing through a region that is one vast slate

quarry, we arrived at Trevena, within fifteen minutes' walk of which is King Arthur's Castle. We lost no time in paying a first visit to it. The castle stands—rather I should say stoops or leans—partly on a projecting cliff, and partly on what is called an island, separated from the cliff by a chasm of twenty or thirty yards breadth. I prefer saying it is separated by a wide chasm. There are various theories as to the original connection between the island and the mainland. The isolated portion, it should be explained, is not properly an island, as the sea never flows between, but it is accessible only by a winding and steep path on the face of a lofty precipice. Some say that the island was once united to the land by a connecting neck, and that the castle occupied the whole way across. Others aver that the island and mainland were quite separate at one time, and were united by a drawbridge: that afterwards the cliff on either side fell down and partially filled up the passage where the sea intervened before, and created the chasm that now exists at the top. So, however, it is that one portion of the castle is on the rock that is nearest to the island, and another portion on the island itself. The two outer walls on either side run towards each other, and would meet if continued across the chasm. The island is between three and four acres in extent. This small space swells, and droops, and undulates, and forms plains, and hills, and vales. It is covered with the thickest and softest carpet of grass that was ever trodden. It is surrounded by a cliff that is terrific in its height and savage outline. The ruins of a small chapel lie on an elevated part, and a shallow grave cut in the rock lies by its side. Entrance to the insular part of the castle is obtained through a gate, the key of which can be got at a cottage not far off, the only condition being that you must lock the door when you have entered, to prevent the sheep, who are always on the watch for an opportunity, from getting in. Having made a hasty inspection we returned, and the next morning set out for a more lengthened exploration. The day was sunny, and soft, and warm; one of those days that seldom come in a lifetime. We got the key and locked ourselves into the island. In attempting to describe the old castle, for some reason unknown to myself, I use the word senility rather than antiquity. The smaller and the humbler the abode, the more closely does it remind us of man. Towering bastions and frowning fortresses have a character and identity of their own, and rank with the sublimities of material nature. The hut, the shed, the fragile walls and roof of thatch are sanctified by the eternal presence of the household gods. This is the order of architecture to which Tintagel belongs. It is ancient beyond history, or tradition, or probable conjectures, and is worn and attenuated to decrepitude by the waste of time. But it will be half human while a stone stands on another. It is hollowed and beaten by rain and wind to a shred, and you sympathize in its decay as with a fellow-mortal. After walking for a while through the ruins, my wife sat on the broken wall of the old chapel, and I set off in search of adventures through the island. All desire to investigate, all power to distinguish or enumerate, were lost in pure enjoyment. Part of the space, where it inclines down to the cliff, is covered with innumerable anthills. From another point, where the base of the rocks is visible, flocks of puffins are seen. I stumbled on an old cave like many which I have seen in my childhood. I found a bird's nest, and looked in at the rounded treasures it contained with suspended breath, as I had done when a boy. I stood on the extreme verge of the mighty cliff, and gazed abroad until consciousness began to blend into vague immensity. Then I looked back at the quiet figure sitting on the ruined chapel in the distance, and the island became home, carpeted with verdure, domed by heaven, walled by infinity, with the distant sound of the cruel world vainly raging without. Then we walked round the cliff together. My wife saw a coin in the rocks—a coin probably dropped by King Arthur. I picked it up and we carefully examined it. It proved to be a semi-denarius of the bronze period of Queen Victoria's reign. I believe the proper owner of it is the Duke of Cornwall. Until it is claimed I am His Royal Highness's vicegerent. We afterwards went through the other part of the castle on the mainland in which the principal gateway stands, with a winding approach to it up the side of a steep hill. One doorway through the thickest part of the wall leading sheer out on a deep precipice perplexed me in vain efforts to imagine its use. It may have been an entrance for goods brought by ships, for the sea was nearly under it.

On our way to the village we sat to take a parting view. As I looked my vision suddenly found its focus, as when the duplicates under the stereoscope join into one, and I distinctly saw a party of gaily caparisoned knights, with pennons flying and armour gleaming in the sunset, riding up the zigzag towards the castle gate. I almost ceased to breathe as I gazed on the sight. Eleven warriors, preceded by a figure of surpassing stature and dignity, moved before me in the yet clear daylight. The castle was no longer in ruins. Its front presented an unbroken battlement, and a flag floated from its highest tower. I soon became conscious that someone seated himself on my right-hand side, my wife being on my left. As well as I could perceive in the bewilderment of the moment, it was an old man with a long white beard, and carrying a singular staff in his hand. "Who are those?" I asked him, scarcely taking my eyes from the strange vision. "Look and see," he answered, at the same time pointing to them with his staff. I looked and saw seven of the wildest-looking rascals I ever beheld, riding mountain horses as wild and shaggy as themselves, with one riding in front, who was certainly, as far as appearances went, the natural leader of such followers. "Is that King Arthur riding first?" I said. "You may call him King Arthur if it pleases you," answered my new acquaintance, "but all the same his real name is McCarthy." "And who is that mild-looking youth that goes just after him?" I inquired. "His name," was the answer, "is Gallagher, but they call him Galahad." "Is not he a very devout young man ?" I said. "He is, as long as you're looking at him, and he knows it, but I won't answer for more than that," was the reply. "Why," said I, "did he not go on a pilgrimage in search of a holy cup, at one time ?" "There would be no occasion at all for the cup to be holy for him to go in search of it," the old man answered. "If there was whisky in it, that would be holiness enough for him." "And who is that rakish fellow," said I, "who wears his helmet in such a jaunty style ?" "His name," said my old friend, "is Larry Toole, but they call him Lancelot for shortness." "Isn't he a rather loose-going kind of youth ?" I asked. "He's not a very particular sort of chap," was the old man's answer, "but I'd a sight sooner trust him than Jim Gallagher." "Don't they sit round a table all equal ?" was my next inquiry. "Faith," said my friend, "if you'll go up to the castle to-night, in the small hours of the morning" (I am repeating his exact words)—"if you'll go up to-night, in the small hours of the morning, it's *under* the table you'll find them all equal, and no mistake." "Could you inform me," I next inquired, "how the island came to be divided from the mainland, or whether it was always so ?" "Well," he answered, "I'll tell you how it came about. A man named Barney Neill rented the island from Arthur, but in a short time he wanted a new valuation and a reduction, and Arthur wouldn't consent to it: so what does Barney do but get a crowbar one night when Arthur and the boys were out, and pulled down the rocks just as you see them. He repealed the union without any doubt. And now he won't pay a penny of rent at all, for he says Arthur is an absentee; and what else could he be but an absentee, when he can't set foot on the island?" "Might I make so bold as to ask your name?" said I. "Well, then, you may," said he; "my name is Murrough O'Lyne." "And may I take the further liberty of inquiring," said I, "whether they call you anything for shortness?" "Why, then, they do," answered he; "they call me Merlin." "Merlin," I gasped, almost breathless with astonishment. And then, in the excitement of the moment, I, with most culpable thoughtlessness and bad taste, asked, "Where's Vivien." "There, now," said Merlin, "that's the way people talk. Look there," continued he, holding out his wand; "look at her just coming out of the gate of the Dune." I looked and saw a dark-haired girl, with graceful figure and elastic step, issue from the castle gate. "Do you see any white samite on her?" asked Merlin. "I must confess my entire ignorance," said I, "of that mystic and wonderful fabric, but I can confidently say that your friend over the way is distinguished rather by its absence than its presence, whatever it be." "Exactly," said Merlin, "and you may judge all the rest by that. Her name, for one thing, is not Vivien at all; her name is Biddy. She's a girl of the Caseys. And there isn't in the whole kingdom of Cornwall an honester or a decenter girl than herself." "How can you go on talking nonsense all night?" said a voice on my left. I turned a meekly remonstrative look in that direction, and when I looked back again, Merlin was gone. The castle was once more in ruins, and where Arthur and his knights had been, a few sheep nibbled the grass.

The moment I got into the hotel I referred to a "History of Tintagel" which lay on the table, and there I read that the castle in ancient days contained stalls for seven horses. This was exactly the number that I saw, according to Merlin's way of putting things. I also read that the old name of Tintagel was Dundagium. "Dagium" is evidently only the Latin termination, so that Dun was the original name of the place. Now "dune" is the Irish word for fort or fortress. It may be remembered that Merlin spoke of Vivien as coming out of the Dune. The place was clearly an Irish fort.

Towards nightfall I went to take one more view of the castle, as we were to leave next morning. I took the road leading to the church, which would bring me to a fresh approach. The day had changed. The sky was dreary, and there was a mournful wail in the wind as it swept over the desolate downs. The iron of pitiless circumstance entered into my soul. The church as I passed it seemed like the tomb of a dead god, with the lesser tombs of his worshippers clustering round. Despair weighed on my spirits ; but it was rather a diffused and passive melancholy than a sharp anguish. I made no struggle, but yielded to the influences that surrounded me, and to the bitter blast that bore me on. The island, with its rent and tortured cliffs, and the aged and decrepit castle came in sight. Sea and wind, wave upon wave, and blast upon blast, without blind rage, without thought of possible failure, beat on the stones that nature had laid and those which man's hand had erected, and wasted away the strength of both alike. Years and years ago I witnessed the spectacle, before unknown to me, of a cat torturing a mouse. The little creature, when tossed into the air by its gigantic executioner, always the instant it fell sat erect on its haunches in defiance and exhibited its tiny teeth. And this unequalled courage and constancy were in vain against the tyranny of fate! But I was wrong, for I stood by, a possible avenger, and I had a gun in my hand. Still I have never forgotten the incident, and it now came back on me as the interpreter of the scene before me. The great torturers, the sea and the storm, were playing with the shore. The cliffs stood in haughty defiance, the buffeted rocks frowned back on their foe. But all was in vain. The calm and cruel monster—calm in its fury and cruel in its repose—was gradually eating away the vitals of its victim. The frown on the brow of the cliff was made only of the wrinkles that ages of tempest had written. The threatening buttresses and tall minarets of stone were only the writhing limbs of a despairing combatant. All was giving way, nothing could endure. Again, the iron chain of material destiny clasped my soul and enthralled it. My consciousness melted into the external world. All nature around, the dismal ocean, the worn rocks, the emaciated ruins, became conscious in my consciousness. I saw them no longer: I was part of them—warring with them, perishing with them.

"The heaven and the earth shall pass away, but My word shall not pass away." No one knows the power of words till they come at the right moment. I recovered and collected my wandering fancies. I saw nature from my human height. My soul, that had evaporated and been the soul of the wind, and wave, and rocks, condensed and crystallized, and looked out from her battlement which the tempest cannot reach; and, like a mass of floating vapour that gathers into a dewdrop, I reflected the outside world instead of mingling with it.

Within a short drive or walk of Trevena, in the valley of Trevillet, is a waterfall called St. Knighton, or St. Nectan's Kieve. On a high rock near the fall stand the walls of a small building where the saint lived. Once on a time, two ladies took up their abode in this building and died in it—no one ever knew whence they came, or their names or histories. This is no uncommon circumstance in Cornwall. A foreigner came to a farmhouse, begged to be taken in as a lodger, paid liberally in gold coins of some other land, entreating his landlord not to exhibit them till he went away or died; never went out by day, and died in a few years unknown even by name. One writer (Hunt) confounds the Kieve, the name of a miner's vessel applied to the basin into which the water falls, with the hermitage. Another (Collins) describes the place where the strange ladies lived and died at a cottage on the outskirts of the wood. The building on the high rock near the fall is of great antiquity. It belongs to a class of small stone-roofed chapels whose origin and use are unknown. One of these stands outside Torquay on the top of a steep precipice. There are one or two in Ireland. If, as is said, they were guides for mariners, it must have been by the aid of perpetually burning lights, and this takes us back to the time when our Aryan forefathers came from the East.

I have only to repair an omission and add that the clergyman and his sweetheart, whom we left wandering around the site of the vanished merry maidens, found each other at last and were married.

THE END.

J. E. CORNISH'S PUBLICATIONS.

Abstracts of some of the Medical and Surgical Cases treated at the Children's Hospital, Pendlebury. Edited by Henry Ashby, M.D., H. R. Hutton, M.B., and G. A. Wright, F.R.C.S. 6th year of issue. 2*s.*

Roger Bacon. The Philosophy of Science in the Middle Ages. By R. Adamson, M.A., LL.D., Professor of Logic in the Owens College, Victoria University. 1*s.*

Aliments for the Sick, by a Lady of much experience in the sick-room. 6*d.*

Art and Hand Work for the People, being three papers read before the Social Science Congress, September, 1884. By Rev. W. Tuckwell, Charles Godfrey Leland, and Walter Besant. 6*d.*

The Physiology and Pathology of Childhood. By Henry Ashby, M.D., Lond., M.R.C.P., Lecturer on Diseases of Children in the Owens College, Victoria University. 6*d.*

The Teaching of Technical Chemistry. By G. H. Bailey, D.Sc., Lecturer on Chemistry in the Owens College, Victoria University. 4*d.*

A Manual of French Pronunciation, as exhibited in ordinary life. By Paul Eug. Ed. Barbier. 1*s.* 6*d.*

Warwick Brookes' Pencil Pictures of Child Life, with Biographical Reminiscences. By T. Letherbrow.

Calendar of the Victoria University. 1*s.*

The Questions of the Bible arranged in the order of the Book of Scripture. By W. Carnelley, with Preface by S. G. Green, D.D. 7*s.* 6*d.*

Illustrations of the Architecture and Archæology of the Cathedral Church of S. Mary the Virgin, S. George, and S. Denys, Manchester. In a series of about 40 plates, with descriptive letterpress. By J. S. Crowther. [In preparation.]

The Criminal Responsibility of the Insane. By C. J. Cullingworth, M.D., F.R.C.P. 6*d.*

Dammann (K.). German Accidence, or the Essentials of German Grammar. 2*s.*

Notes on Artillery. By Charles C. du Pré, F.L.S., late Captain 3rd Middlesex A. Volunteers, and the Manchester Artillery. 6*d.*

Greek Exercises for Beginners. Translated from the Greek Grammar of Professor George Curtius. By Edwin B. England, M.A., Lecturer in Greek and Latin in the Owens College, Victoria University. 1*s.*

The Character and Times of Thomas Cromwell; a criticism of the first ten years of the English Reformation. By Arthur Galton, New Coll., Oxon. Author of 'Urbana Scripta.' 7*s.* 6*d.*

Four Place Logarithmic and Tangent Tables, for the use of Physical, Electrical, Engineering, and Chemical Students. Arranged by W. W. Haldane Gee, B.Sc., Lond., Assistant Lecturer in Physics in the Owens College, Victoria University. 9*d.*

Fasciculus: A Song-Bundle. By H. Hailstone, M.A. 2*s.*

Sertum: A Song-Garland. By H. Hailstone, M.A. 2*s.*

David Westren. By Alfred Hayes, M.A., New Coll., Oxon. 6*s.*

The Last Crusade and other Poems. By Alfred Hayes, M.A., New Coll., Oxon. 6*s.* 6*d.*

Life and Correspondence of Samuel Hibbert Ware, M.D., F.R.S.E., etc. Edited by Mrs. Hibbert Ware. With a Portrait of Dr. Hibbert Ware. 21*s.*

Easements and Rights of Light. By John Holden, F.R.I.B.A., F.S.I. 3*s.*

The Faculty of Laws and the Idea of Law. By Alfred Hopkinson, B.C.L., M.A., Professor of Law in the Owens College, Victoria University. *6d.*

Hunting Maps. **Cheshire, Wynnstay, and North Staffordshire Hunts.** Mounted on cloth and folded in case for the pocket. *4s.* each.

Hymns and Sacred Songs for Sunday Schools and Public Worship. *8d.*; or cloth, gilt edges, *10d.*

Decorative Design: An Elementary Text Book of Principles and Practice. By Frank Jackson, Second Master in the Birmingham Municipal School of Art. *7s. 6d.*

Diseases of the Bones, their Pathology, Diagnosis, and Treatment. By Thomas Jones, F.R.C.S., B.S., Lecturer on Practical Surgery in the Owens College, Victoria University. With illustrations. *12s. 6d.*

The Instantaneous Chest Squarer, or Case Maker's Ready Reckoner. By Oliver C. Kenyon. 2nd Edition. *6s.*

Caer Pensauelcoit, A Long Lost un-Romanised British Metropolis. Occasioned by two Reports of an Exploration Committee of the Somersetshire Archæological and Natural History Society, having for Assessors, Professor Boyd-Dawkins, General A. Pitt-Rivers, and Professor Rolleston. By Thomas Kerslake, 1882. With Map. *1s.*

The Liberty of Independent Historical Research. By Thomas Kerslake, 1885. *1s.*

The Origins of Geometry. By Horace Lamb, M.A., F.R.S., Professor of Pure Mathematics in the Owens College, Victoria University. *6d.*

The Relation of Pharmacology to Therapeutics. By D. J. Leech, M.D., F.R.C.P., Professor of Materia Medica and Therapeutics in the Owens College, Victoria University. *6d.*

The Present Position of the Antiseptic Question; being the substance of the oration for the year 1883, delivered before the Medical Society of London. By Edward Lund, F.R.C.S., Professor of Surgery in the Owens College, Victoria University. *2s.*

Five Years' Surgical Work in the Manchester Royal Infirmary. By Edward Lund, F.R.C.S. *3s.*

Observations on some of the more recent Methods of Treating Wounds, and on Excision of the Knee-joint. By Edward Lund, F.R.C.S. *2s.*

Palliative Medicine and Palliative Treatment in Surgical Cases. By Edward Lund, F.R.C.S. *6d.*

The Removal of the Entire Tongue by the Walter Whitehead Method, with full details of the operation and after-treatment, by Edward Lund, F.R.C.S. *2s.*

MANCHESTER TACTICAL SOCIETY PUBLICATIONS.

1.—**Suggestions for a New Field** Exercise for the Volunteer Infantry. By Spencer Wilkinson, Captain 20th L.R.V. 6d.

2.—**Volunteer Artillery.** **Essays** by R. K. Birley, Major and Hon. Lieutenant-Colonel the Manchester Artillery. *6d.*

3.—**English Drill: A Historical** Sketch. By J. L. Aspland, Lieutenant-Colonel 20th L.R.V. *6d.*

4.—**Essays on the War Game.** By Spencer Wilkinson, Captain 20th L.R.V. 1s.

5.—**Exercises in Strategy and** Tactics. Translated from the German by Spencer Wilkinson, Captain 20th L.R.V. With 3 Maps. *2s. 6d.*

6.—**War-Game Maps.** By Henry T. Crook, C.E., Captain 1st Lancashire Engineer Volunteers. *6d.*

7.—**Field Artillery for Home Service.** By R. K. Birley, Major and Hon. Lieutenant-Colonel the Manchester Artillery. *6d.*

8.—**The Conduct of Infantry Fire** according to the French Regulations of 1888. Translated, with an Introduction, by A. P. Ledward, late Captain 20th L.R.V. *6d.*

9.—**Map Manœuvres. An Elementary** Account of the War Game. By A. G. Haywood, Captain 6th V.B. Lancashire Division, R.A. 6*d*.

10.—**Exercises in Strategy and Tactics.** Second Series. By H. von Gizycki, Colonel-Commandant of the 18th (Brandenburg) Field Artillery Regiment. Translated by Henry L. Rocca, Lieutenant-Colonel and Hon. Colonel-Commandant 5th V.B. the Manchester Regiment. 1*s*.

Manchester as it is, a Series of Views. By Alfred Brothers, F.R.A.S., with an Introduction by James Croston, F.S.A. £2 2*s*.

Manchester Court Leet Records from 1552 (with an interval of about 43 years) to 1846. Edited by J. P. Earwaker, F.S.A. Vols. I. to VI., £3 3*s*. net; single volumes, 12*s*. 6*d*. each net. The entire work will be completed in about 12 volumes.

The Frog: an Introduction to Anatomy and Histology. With a Chapter on Development added. By A. Milnes Marshall, M.D., D.Sc., F.R.S., Professor of Biology in the Owens College, Victoria University. 3rd Edition, revised and illustrated. 4*s*.

Owens College: Studies from the Biological Laboratories. Vol. I. Published by the Council of the College, and edited by Professor Milnes Marshall. 10*s*.

Mason Science College Calendar (Birmingham). 1*s*.

Medical Education at the Universities. By J. E. Morgan, M.D., M.A., Professor of Medicine in the Owens College, Victoria University. 1*s*.

The Study of Law in Greece, Rome, and England. By J. E. Crawford Munro, LL.M., LL.D., Professor of Political Economy in the Owens College, Victoria University. 6*d*.

Essays in Literature and Ethics. By the late Rev. William Anderson O'Conor, B.A. Edited, with a Biographical Introduction, by William E. A. Axon. 3*s*. 6*d*.

Old Manchester: a Series of Views of the more Ancient Buildings in Manchester and its vicinity, as they appeared fifty years ago. Drawn by Ralston, James, and others, and reproduced by the Autotype process by Alfred Brothers, F.R.A.S., with an Introduction by James Croston, F.S.A. £2 5*s*.

Owens College Calendar. 3*s*.

Address delivered at the Opening of the Session, Department of Medicine, Owens College, 1887-8. By Sir James Paget, Bart., LL.D., D.C.L., F.R.S. 6*d*.

The Limits of the Infectiveness of Tubercle. By Arthur Ransome, M.D., M.A., Lecturer on Public Health and Hygiene in the Owens College, Victoria University. 6*d*.

The Present Position of State Medicine in England. By Arthur Ransome, M.D., M.A., Lecturer on Public Health and Hygiene in the Owens College, Victoria University. 1*s*.

Engineering: Syllabus of the Lectures at the Owens College, together with a Series of Examples relating to the various Subjects included in the Course. By Osborne Reynolds, M.A., F.R.S., Professor of Engineering in the Owens College, Victoria University. Arranged by J. B. Millar, M.E., Assistant Lecturer in Engineering. 2nd Edition. 3s.

On Spontaneous Generation and the Doctrine of Contagium Vivum. By Sir William Roberts, M.D., F.R.S. 2*s*.

A Selection of Hymns for the Use of Young Persons, and especially for the Children of Sunday Schools. By W. Roby. 8*d*.

Description of the Chemical Laboratories at the Owens College, from the Plans of Alfred Waterhouse, R.A. By Sir H. E. Roscoe, F.R.S. With lithographic copies of the original Plans and Elevations. 5*s*.

On Technical Education. By James Ross, M.D., LL.D., Professor of Medicine in the Owens College, Victoria University. 6*d*.

Notes on the Diagnosis of the various Forms of Paralysis of the Muscles of External Relation. By James Ross, M.D., LL.D., Professor of Medicine in the Owens College, Victoria University. 1*s*.

Inductive Political Economy. By William Lucas Sargant, Author of 'The Science of Social Opulence.' 10*s*. 6*d*.

Contributions to Practical Medicine. By Sir James Sawyer, M.D., Lond., F.R.C.P., Senior Physician to the Queen's Hospital, Birmingham. 6*s*. 6*d*.

Lectures on the Treatment of the Common Diseases of the Skin. By Robert M. Simon, M.D., Cantab., M.R.C.P., Lond., Senior Assistant Physician to the General Hospital, Birmingham. 3*s*.

Reminiscences of Manchester Fifty Years Ago. By J. T. Slugg, F.R.A.S. 4*s*.

The Mechanism of Nature. By Alfred M. Stapley. 1*s*.; cloth, 1*s*. 6*d*.

The Physical Signs of Pulmonary Disease. By Graham Steell, M.D., Lecturer on Clinical Medicine in the Owens College, Victoria University. 3*s*. 6*d*.

The Physical Signs of Cardiac Disease. By Graham Steell, M.D., Lecturer on Clinical Medicine in the Owens College, Victoria University. 2*s*. 6*d*.

Poems. By Henry Septimus Sutton. 6*s*.; large paper, 15*s*.

Diseases of Women. By Lawson Tait, F.R.C.S., LL.D., President of the British Gynæcological Society. 6*s*.

Tariff of Medical Fees issued by the Manchester Medico-Ethical Association. 3rd Edition. 6*d*.

Old Halls of Lancashire and Cheshire, including Notes on the Ancient Domestic Architecture of the Counties Palatine. By Henry Taylor. Numerous Illustrations. £2 10*s*.

The Owens College: its Foundation and Growth, and its Connection with the Victoria University, Manchester. By Joseph Thompson. 18*s*.; large paper, £2 2*s*.

Vaccination: a condensed Summary of the Evidence in its favour, and of the Objections urged against it. By J. Thorburn, M.D. 6*d*.

University College of Wales Calendar. (Aberystwyth.) 1*s*. 6*d*.

University College of North Wales Calendar. (Bangor.) 1*s*. 6*d*.

Pen-and-Ink Drawings for Young Folks. By William Walker. Cloth, 2*s*. 6*d*.; paper, 1*s*. 6*d*.

Histological Notes for the Use of Medical Students. By W. Horscraft Waters, M.A., late Lecturer in the Owens College, Victoria University. 2*s*. 6*d*.

Excision of the Tongue. By Walter Whitehead, F.R.C.S.E., F.R.S., Edin., Lecturer on Clinical Surgery in the Owens College, Victoria University. 1*s*.

The Study of Greek Literature. By A. S. Wilkins, M.A., LL.D., Professor of Latin in the Owens College, Victoria University. 6*d*.

Arithmetical Chemistry; or, Arithmetical Exercises for Chemical Students. By C. J. Woodward, B.Sc. Part I. 1s. Part II. 2s.

Questions in Chemistry and Natural Philosophy, given at the Matriculation Examination of the University of London, from 1864 to 1882, by C. J. Woodward, B.Sc. New Edition, with Answers. 2*s*.

Arithmetical Physics, Acoustics, Light, and Heat. By C. J. Woodward, B.Sc. Part I*a*, Elementary Stage, 2*s*. Part II*a*, 1*s*. Part II*b*, 3*s*.

Arithmetical Physics, Magnetism, and Electricity. By C. J. Woodward, B.Sc. Part II*a*, Elementary Stage, 1*s*. Part II*b*, 3*s*.

A B C Five Figure Logarithms; or, Logarithms with Differences, on a new and simple plan, together with Analytical Factors, Gas, Reduction Tables, etc. By C. J. Woodward, B.Sc. 2*s*. 6*d*.

www.ingramcontent.com/pod-product-compliance
Lightning Source LLC
Chambersburg PA
CBHW030346270326
41926CB00009B/987

* 9 7 8 3 3 3 7 0 1 0 4 6 1 *